Grammar and punctuation

Teacher's Resource Book

TERMS AND CONDITIONS

IMPORTANT – PERMITTED USE AND WARNINGS – READ CAREFULLY BEFORE USING

This CD-ROM has been tested for viruses at all stages of its production. However, we recommend that you run virus-checking software on your computer systems at all times. Scholastic Ltd cannot accept any responsibility for any loss, disruption or damage to your data or your computer system that may occur as a result of using either the CD-ROM or the data held on it.

IF YOU ACCEPT THE ABOVE CONDITIONS YOU MAY PROCEED TO USE THE CD-ROM.

Recommended system requirements:

Windows: XP (Service Pack 3), Vista (Service Pack 2), Windows 7 or Windows 8 with 2.33GHz processor
Mac: OS 10.6 to 10.8 with Intel Core™ Duo processor
1GB RAM (recommended)
1024 x 768 Screen resolution
CD-ROM drive (24x speed recommended)
Adobe Reader (version 9 recommended for Mac users)
Broadband internet connections (for installation and updates)

For all technical support queries (including no CD drive), please phone Scholastic Customer Services on 0845 6039091.

Author
Huw Thomas and Paul Hollin

Editorial team
Rachel Morgan, Melissa Somers, Jenny Wilcox, Tracy Kewley, Gemma Cary, Red Door Media and Margaret Eaton

Series designers
Shelley Best and Anna Oliwa

Design team
Nicolle Thomas and Neil Salt

Illustrations
Simon Walmesley

CD-ROM development
Hannah Barnett, Phil Crothers and MWA Technologies Private Ltd

Designed using Adobe Indesign
Published by Scholastic Ltd,
Book End, Range Road, Witney,
Oxfordshire OX29 0YD
www.scholastic.co.uk

Printed by Ashford Colour Press

1 2 3 4 5 6 7 8 9 5 6 7 8 9 0 1 2 3 4

British Library Cataloguing-in-Publication Data
A catalogue record for this book is available from the British Library.
ISBN 978-1407-14066-7

MIX
Paper from responsible sources
FSC® C011748

Acknowledgements

The publishers gratefully acknowledge permission to reproduce the following copyright material:

David Higham Associates for the use of an extract from *Fantastic Mr Fox* by Roald Dahl. Text © 1970 Roald Dahl Nominee Ltd (1970, George Allen & Unwin).
Walker Books for the use of an extract from *Where's My Teddy?* written and illustrated by Jez Alborough. Text © 1992, Jez Alborough (1992, Walker Books), for the use of an extract from *Owl Babies* by Martin Waddell and illustrated by Patrick Benson. Text © 1992, Martin Waddell (1992, Walker Books) and for the use of an extract from *Farmer Duck* by Martin Waddell and illustrated by Helen Oxenbury. Text ©1991, Martin Waddell (1991, Walker Books). Reproduced by permission of Walker Books Ltd, London SE11 5HJ www.walker.co.uk

Every effort has been made to trace copyright holders for the works reproduced in this book, and the publishers apologise for any inadvertent omissions.

Extracts from *The National Curriculum in English, English Programme of Study* © Crown Copyright. Reproduced under the terms of the Open Government Licence (OGL). http://www.nationalarchives.gov.uk/doc/open-government-licence/open-government-licence.htm

Contents

INTRODUCTION 4

CURRICULUM OBJECTIVES 7

Chapter 1

Pronouns

INTRODUCTION 9
NOUNS 12
PRONOUNS 16
PRONOUNS TAKE THEIR PLACE 20
PRONOUNS IN TEXT 24
PRONOUNS IN WRITING 28

Chapter 2

Words at work

INTRODUCTION 32
WORD CLASSES 35
FORMING NOUNS 39
INDEFINITE ARTICLES 43
WORD FAMILIES 47
WORDSMITHS 51

Chapter 3

Verbs and tenses

INTRODUCTION 55
REVIEWING VERBS 58
VERB TENSES 62
WRITING ABOUT THE PAST 66
TENSE SPOTTING 70
VERBS IN WRITING 74

Chapter 4

Sentences

INTRODUCTION 78
CLAUSES 81
LINKING CLAUSES 85
CONJUNCTIONS, ADVERBS AND PREPOSITIONS 89
SHOWING TIME, PLACE AND CAUSE 93
IMPROVING SENTENCE WRITING 97

Chapter 5

Organising texts

INTRODUCTION 101
WHAT IS A PARAGRAPH? 104
USING PARAGRAPHS 108
HEADINGS AND SUBHEADINGS 112
ORGANISING NON-NARRATIVE WRITING 116
PLANNING AND ORGANISING WRITING 120

Chapter 6

Apostrophes and inverted commas

INTRODUCTION 124
APOSTROPHES TO SHOW POSSESSION 127
USING POSSESSIVE APOSTROPHES WITH PLURALS 131
WHAT ARE THEY SAYING? 135
INVERTED COMMAS AND DIRECT SPEECH 139
PUNCTUATION IN WRITING 143

SUBJECT KNOWLEDGE 147

Introduction

Scholastic English Skills: Grammar and punctuation

This series is based on the premise that grammar and punctuation can be interesting and dynamic – but on one condition. The condition is that the teaching of these grammar aspects must be related to real texts and practical activities that experiment with language, investigate the use of language in realistic contexts and find the ways in which grammar and punctuation are used in our day-to-day speech, writing and reading. This book encourages children to look back at their written work and find ways to revise and improve it.

Teaching grammar and punctuation

'As a writer I know that I must select studiously the nouns, pronouns, verbs, adverbs, etcetera, and by a careful syntactical arrangement make readers laugh, reflect or riot.'

Maya Angelou

The *Scholastic English Skills: Grammar and punctuation* series equips teachers with resources and subject training to enable them to teach grammar and punctuation effectively. The focus of the resource is on what is sometimes termed 'sentence-level work', so called because grammar and punctuation primarily involve the construction and understanding of sentences.

Many teachers bring with them a lot of past memories when they approach the teaching of grammar. Some will remember school grammar lessons as the driest of subjects, involving drills and parsing, and will wonder how they can make it exciting for their own class. At the other end of the spectrum, some will have received relatively little formal teaching of grammar at school. In other words, there are teachers who, when asked to teach clause structure or prepositions, feel at a bit of a loss. They are being asked expectantly to teach things they are not confident with themselves.

Grammar can evoke lethargy, fear, irritation, pedantry and despondency. Yet as demonstrated by the above comment from Maya Angelou, even one of our greatest modern writers presents her crafting of sentences as an exciting and tactical process that has a powerful effect on her readers. Can this be the grammar that makes teachers squirm or run?

About the product

The book is divided into six chapters. Each chapter looks at a different aspect of grammar and punctuation and is divided into sections. Each section includes teachers' notes – objective, background knowledge, notes on how to use the photocopiable pages, further ideas and digital content – and up to three photocopiable pages.

Posters

Each chapter has two posters. These posters are related to the contents of the chapter and should be displayed and used for reference throughout the work on the chapter. The poster notes (on the chapter introduction page) offer suggestions for how they could be used. There are black and white versions in the book and full-colour versions on the CD-ROM for you to print out or display on your whiteboard.

Activities

Each section contains three activities. These activities all take the form of a photocopiable page which is in the book. Each photocopiable page is also included on the CD-ROM for you to display or print out (answers are also provided, where appropriate, in a separate document on the CD-ROM).

Many of the photocopiable pages have linked interactive activities on the CD-ROM. These interactive activities are designed to act as starter activities to the lesson, giving whole-class support on the information being taught. However, they can also work equally well as plenary activities, reviewing the work the children have just completed.

Workbooks

Accompanying this series is a set of workbooks containing practice activities which are divided into chapters to match the teacher's resource book. Use a combination of the photocopiable pages in this book and the activities in the workbook to help children practise and consolidate grammar and punctuation skills.

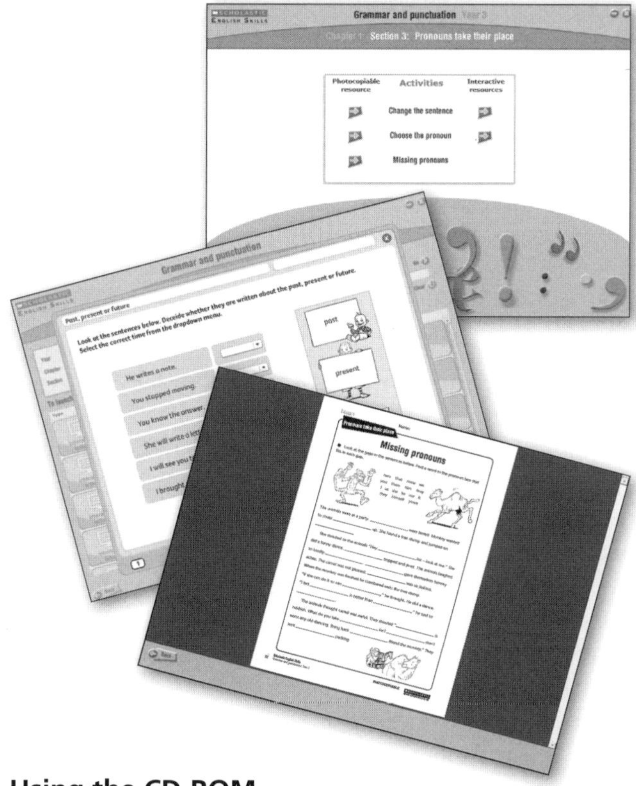

Using the CD-ROM

Below are brief guidance notes for using the CD-ROM. For more detailed information, see 'How to use this digital content' on the Main menu.

The CD-ROM follows the structure of the book and contains:

- All of the photocopiable pages.
- All of the poster pages in full colour.
- Answers provided, where relevant.
- Interactive on-screen activities linked to the photocopiable pages.

Getting started

Put the CD-ROM into your CD-ROM drive.

- For Windows users, the install wizard should autorun, if it fails to do so then navigate to your CD-ROM drive. Then follow the installation process.
- For Mac users, copy the disk image file to your hard drive. After it has finished copying double click it to mount the disk image. Navigate to the mounted disk image and run the installer. After installation the disk image can be unmounted and the DMG can be deleted from the hard drive.
- To install on a network, please see the ReadMe file located on the CD-ROM (navigate to your drive).

To complete the installation of the program you need to open the program and click 'Update' in the pop-up. Please note – this CD-ROM is web-enabled and the content will be downloaded from the internet to your hard-drive to populate the CD-ROM with the relevant resources. This only needs to be done on first use, after this you will be able to use the CD-ROM without an internet connection. If at any point any content is updated you will receive another pop-up upon start up with an internet connection.

Main menu

The main menu is the first screen that appears. Here you can access: terms and conditions, registration links, how to use the CD-ROM and credits. To access a specific year group click on the relevant button (NB only titles installed will be available). To browse all installed content click **All resources**.

Chapter menu

The Chapter menu provides links to all of the chapters or all of the resources for a specific year group. Clicking on the relevant Chapter icon will take you to the section screen where you can access the posters and the chapter's sections. Clicking on **All resources** will take you to a list of all the resources, where you can search by keyword or chapter for a specific resource.

Section menu

Here you can choose the relevant section to take you to its activity screen. You can also access the posters here.

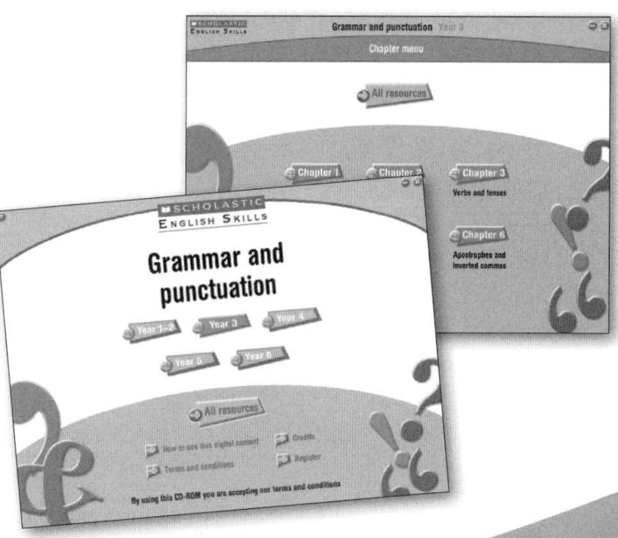

Activity menu

Upon choosing a section from the section menu, you are taken to a list of resources for that section. Here you can access all of the photocopiable pages related to that section as well as the linked interactive activities.

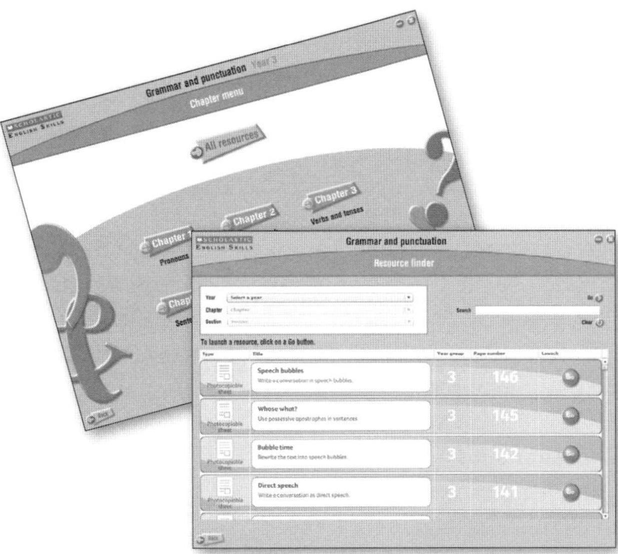

All resources

All resources lists all of the resources for a year group (if accessed via a Chapter menu) or all of the installed resources (if accessed via the Main menu). You can:

- Select a chapter and/or section by selecting the appropriate title from the drop-down menus.
- Search for key words by typing them into the search box.
- Scroll up or down the list of resources to locate the required resource.
- To launch a resource, simply click on the **Go** button.

Navigation

The resources (poster pages, photocopiable pages and interactive activities) all open in separate windows on top of the menu screen. To close a resource, click on the **x** in the top right-hand corner of the screen and this will return you to the menu screen.

Closing a resource will not close the program. However, if you are in a menu screen, then clicking on the **x** will close the program. To return to a previous menu screen, you need to click on the **Back** button.

Teacher settings

In the top left-hand corner of the Main menu screen is a small **T** icon. This is the teacher settings area. It is password protected, the password is: login. This area will allow you to choose the print quality settings for interactive activities 'Default' or 'Best'. It will also allow you to check for updates to the program or re-download all content to the disk via **Refresh all content**.

Answers

The answers to the photocopiable pages can be found on the CD-ROM in the All resources menu. The answers are supplied in one document in a table-format, referencing the page number, title and answer for each relevant page. The pages that have answers are referenced in the 'Digital content' boxes on the teachers' notes pages. Unfortunately, due to the nature of English, not all pages can have answers provided because some activities require the children's own imaginative input or consist of a wider writing task.

Objectives

	Page	Section	English skills objective	To choose nouns or pronouns appropriately for clarity and cohesion and to avoid repetition.	To form nouns using a range of prefixes.	To use the forms 'a' or 'an' according to whether the next word begins with a vowel.	To recognise word families based on common words, showing how words are related in form and meaning.	To extend the range of sentences with more than one clause by using a wider range of conjunctions, including *when, if, because, although.*	To use the present perfect form of verbs in contrast to the past tense.
Chapter 1	12	Nouns	To revisit nouns.	✓					
	16	Pronouns	To recognise and identify pronouns.	✓					
	20	Pronouns take their place	To choose pronouns appropriately.	✓					
	24	Pronouns in text	To investigate the use of pronouns.	✓					
	28	Pronouns in writing	To extend the use of pronouns in writing.	✓					
Chapter 2	35	Word classes	To revise nouns and adjectives, verbs and adverbs.	✓					
	39	Forming nouns	To form nouns using a range of prefixes.		✓				
	43	Indefinite articles	To use 'a' and 'an' accurately.			✓			
	47	Word families	To explore how words can be related in form and meaning.				✓		
	51	Wordsmiths	To develop the use of new knowledge and vocabulary.	✓	✓	✓	✓		
Chapter 3	58	Reviewing verbs	To recognise and understand the function of verbs in sentences.					✓	
	62	Verb tenses	To understand and use verb tenses correctly.					✓	
	66	Writing about the past	To understand that there are different ways of writing about events that have already happened.					✓	✓
	70	Tense spotting	To use different verb tenses in writing.					✓	✓
	74	Verbs in writing	To develop the use of verbs and verb tenses in writing.					✓	✓

Objectives

	Page	Section	English skills objective	To extend the range of sentences with more than one clause by using a wider range of conjunctions, including *when, if, because, although*.	To use conjunctions, adverbs and prepositions to express time and cause.	To use paragraphs as a way to group related material and organise around a theme.	To use headings and subheadings to aid presentation.	**To indicate possession by using the possessive apostrophe with singular and plural nouns.**	To know the grammatical difference between plural and possessive 's'.	To use and punctuate direct speech.
Chapter 4	**81**	Clauses	To identify clauses.	✓						
	85	Linking clauses	To use a range of conjunctions.	✓						
	89	Conjunctions, adverbs and prepositions	To understand the function of conjunctions, adverbs and prepositions.	✓	✓					
	93	Showing time, place and cause	To express time, place and cause.		✓					
	97	Improving sentence writing	To improve sentence writing by incorporating conjunctions, adverbs and prepositions.	✓	✓					
Chapter 5	**104**	What is a paragraph?	To understand how paragraphs are used to group related material.			✓				
	108	Using paragraphs	To begin to use paragraphs in writing.			✓				
	112	Headings and subheadings	To understand how headings and subheadings can be used to organise information.				✓			
	116	Organising non-narrative writing	To begin to use simple organisational devices in writing.			✓	✓			
	120	Planning and organising writing	To use paragraphs and other organisational devices in writing.			✓	✓			
Chapter 6	**127**	Apostrophes to show possession	To revisit apostrophes to mark singular possession in nouns.					✓	✓	
	131	Using possessive apostrophes with plurals	To use apostrophes to mark plural possession in nouns.					✓	✓	
	135	What are they saying?	To identify the words spoken by characters.							✓
	139	Inverted commas and direct speech	To understand that in direct speech spoken words are indicated using inverted commas							✓
	143	Punctuation in writing	To use apostrophes and inverted commas in writing.					✓	✓	✓

Chapter 1

Pronouns

Introduction

This chapter focuses on pronouns and the role they perform in substituting for nouns. After revising the meaning and use of nouns, the activities introduce and look at different pronouns, considering the 'person' they represent and how they develop clarity and cohesion in texts and writing. Throughout the chapter there is an emphasis on exploring these grammatical features in real contexts – such as texts, comics and conversations. For further practice, please see the 'Pronouns' section of the Year 3 workbook.

Poster notes

Pronouns (page 10)
This poster presents the various words that can function as personal pronouns. They are organised into rows of singular and plural pronouns. The poster provides an opportunity for children to think of sentences where they would use particular pronouns.
Person (page 11)
The same pronouns are organised into the first, second and third person. Use the poster to help children appreciate the use of different 'persons' in writing.

- First-person pronouns: identify with the speaker or writer, either alone ('I swam', 'my lunch') or as part of a group ('we swam', 'our house').
- Second-person pronouns: identify with the one being addressed in speech or writing ('you must remember', 'your bike').
- Third-person pronouns: identify with a third party or thing who is neither the one addressing nor the one addressed ('her book', 'he shouted').

In this chapter

Nouns page 12	To revisit nouns.
Pronouns page 16	To recognise and identify pronouns.
Pronouns take their place page 20	To choose pronouns appropriately.
Pronouns in text page 24	To investigate the use of pronouns.
Pronouns in writing page 28	To extend the use of pronouns in writing.

Vocabulary

Children should already know:
noun
In Year 3 children need to know:
pronoun

Pronouns

Pronouns

I	me	my	mine	myself
you	you	your	yours	yourself
he	him	his	his	himself
she	her	her	hers	herself
we	us	our	ours	ourselves
they	them	their	theirs	themselves

Pronouns

Person

First person
I
me
my
mine
myself
we
us
our
ours
ourselves

Second person
you
your
yours
yourself
yourselves

Third person
he
him
his
himself
she
her
hers
herself
they
them
their
theirs
themselves

Nouns

Objective

To revisit nouns.

Background knowledge

Nouns are words that name concrete things or abstract thoughts and feelings. This class of words includes all words that can act as subjects in a sentence, so if a word can follow the articles 'a', 'an' or 'the' in a sentence then it is a noun. This means that words like 'walk', which would commonly be classed as a verb, can be classed as a noun in a sentence like *We are going for a walk.* The verb here is 'going', because that is the action 'we' are taking. Nouns can often be detected by the way they can be turned from singular to plural and vice versa. In this example 'we' could go for a number of 'walks': *We are going for a few walks.* Although the plurals made may seem odd, the pluralisation rule acts as another useful test for most nouns, excluding irregular plurals such as 'mice' and non-countable nouns such as 'sugar'.

Activities

- **Photocopiable page 13 'Is this a noun?'**
In applying the 'a', 'an' or 'the' test, children can be asked to think of a context in which a construction can work. It is difficult to think of an example in which we would say 'a soft' but we can imagine talking about 'a jump' in a context like *She did a brilliant jump.* This helps us to determine which of these two words could be used as a noun.
- **Photocopiable page 14 'Finding nouns'**
As children swap the nouns around in this activity, they will need to check that the sentences they make include consistent uses of single and plural nouns, as well as punctuation.
- **Photocopiable page 15 'Missing words'**
In each of the sentences on the photocopiable sheet there is a range of nouns that could be used to fill the spaces. Children can work in twos and threes to come up with a list of possibilities for each of the spaces. They can then think about how some of their chosen alternatives could be used in a short story idea, which they can plan together.

Further ideas

- **Headlines:** Look at the headlines of newspaper stories. Ask the children to find words that are used as nouns in the headlines but could be used as verbs in a different sentence, for example: *Talks crumble in union row*. They can cut out the words and create the new sentence around them.
- **Dictionary nouns:** Taking any page in the dictionary, ask the children to go through the words listed, testing them to see if they could be used as nouns.
- **Jumble sentences:** Ask the children to take several sentences from a story and jumble the nouns around to make a nonsensical opening.

Digital content

On the digital component you will find:

- Printable versions of all three photocopiable pages.
- Answers to 'Is this a noun?'.
- Interactive version of 'Is this a noun?'.

Nouns

Is this a noun?

A noun is a word for a thing.

It could be an abstract thing you just know. For example: An understanding.

It could be a thing you see.

■ Sort these words into **two** separate lists:
- words we could use as nouns
- words we don't use as nouns.

heard	child	can	always	dog
can't	happy	sure	apple	sound
flat	until	swim	soft	where
jump	light	egg	word	stopped

Name:

Nouns

Finding nouns

■ Cut out the nouns from these sentences and swap them round to make new sentences. For example:

Please pass the sugar

and

Don't feed the tiger

Please pass the	tiger

Could be cut and pasted into:

Don't feed the	sugar

Please pass the sugar.
Can I eat a biscuit?
Don't feed the tiger.
The rain is heavy, use this umbrella.
Quick! Pass me the fire extinguisher.
Could I borrow your handkerchief?
You can throw those sweet wrappers in the bin.
I put your dirty socks and pants in the laundry basket.

Nouns

Missing words

■ Collect a list of words which could fit in the sentences below. Write them in the appropriate boxes.

■ Choose the best words and write the complete sentences on the lines below.

The [ ] fell off the [ ].

The [ ] found a [ ].

The [ ] escaped from a [ ].

The [ ] was chased by a [ ].

The [ ] discovered a secret [ ].

The noisy [ ] disturbed the [ ].

Silently, we entered the [ ].

"Look out, it's a [ ]."

Pronouns

Objective

To recognise and identify pronouns.

Background knowledge

Pronouns are words that are substituted for nouns or noun phrases. In the sentence *Joe gave the cake to Samia*, the noun 'Joe' can be substituted for the pronoun 'he' to make *He gave the cake to Samia*. The other nouns, 'the cake' and 'Samia', can also be substituted to make *He gave it to her*.

Pronouns are relatively anonymous words. In the above example 'Joe' may be a particular person but 'he' could refer to any one of half the population. Similarly 'the cake' is more definite than 'it'. When pronouns are used they tend to require a shared understanding of who or what they refer to.

Pronouns are used in place of nouns but, unlike nouns, they cannot be modified by adjectives. So whereas the usage *He gave the delicious cake to her* is straightforward, the sentence *He gave the delicious it to her* isn't. The only way of using an adjective here would be to use the construction 'the… one', as in 'the delicious one' – but this implies a further meaning that there is 'one' that isn't delicious.

Activities

- **Photocopiable page 17 'Who is you?'**

This activity takes children through a text that is artificially inflated with pronouns. This gives children an idea of the way such words function. One way of reading the text is for children to imagine the pronouns as words that are pointing and, as they read them, to ask: *Who am I pointing at as I say this word?* The idea of pointing as they say 'we' or 'that' should enhance the way the pronouns work in this text.

- **Photocopiable page 18 'Pronouns in action'**

As the children work through this activity they will need a variety of texts. You may find it useful to skim-read the texts beforehand to check which pronouns they contain. The children may also use texts they bring from home in which they have noticed pronouns.

- **Photocopiable page 19 'Awkward sentences'**

As children read the sentences in this activity they are asked to alter the ones that sound 'awkward'. This may provide an opportunity to discuss the redrafting or editing process that takes place in the production of texts and ask children to imagine they are undertaking this task.

Further ideas

- **Exhaustive list:** The pronoun family is not vast. Children may be able to compile an exhaustive list. As they read through various texts they can put forward examples they find of words that may be pronouns. The class can consider whether or not they are and, if so, add them to the list.
- **Customise 'you':** Once they have tried photocopiable page 17, 'Who is you?', the children can try to produce their own example using a text. They can isolate the pronouns and note the questions the reader needs to answer in order to understand the pronoun being used.

Digital content

On the digital component you will find:

- Printable versions of all three photocopiable pages.
- Answers to all three photocopiable pages.
- Interactive version of 'Awkward sentences'.

Pronouns

Who is you?

- Look at the story below. It includes the following pronouns:

you	them	him	our
us	yourself	she	we
he	that	those	they
her	it	herself	

- These words refer to someone or something. They stand in for a noun (the name of something).
- Who or what does each of the pronouns in the story refer to? The pronouns are the words shown in bold type. Write the noun referred to above each pronoun.

Monty and Natasha's walk

Natasha took Monty, **her** dog, for their afternoon walk.

He didn't like being on **his** lead so **he** pulled and pulled at **it**. Natasha let **him** lead the way. As **they** walked **she** chatted to **herself**.

"Where are **you** taking **us**?" **she** asked Monty.

They came to the park.

"**We** can stop here if **you** like," **she** said. "**We** don't need to be home for **our** tea yet."

She found a stick and threw **it**.

"Can you chase **that**?" **she** said. Monty found **it**.

Then **she** threw two sticks. "OK" **she** shouted, "Chase **those**."

She threw **them** as far as **she** could. **They** landed up in a tree!

"Fetch **them yourself**," Monty growled.

Name:

Pronouns in action

■ Gather together a range of texts. You could look in picture books, a newspaper, an advert, a letter… any texts you choose.

■ Look in each of your texts for the pronouns below. When you find an example fill in the chart below.

I me my mine myself you yours yourself he him his himself she her hers herself we us our ours ourselves they them their theirs it its itself this these that those

■ Write the pronouns in the pronoun column below.

■ Next to the pronoun write the person or thing it stands in for.

Pronoun	What the pronoun stands in for (the noun)

Awkward sentences

Some of the nouns in these sentences don't need to be there.

Dave found Dave's coat.

They could be taken away: Dave found ~~Dave~~'s coat.

and pronouns could be put in their place: Dave found his coat.

■ Replace the bold nouns with pronouns. Write the correct pronoun above each of the bold words.

them they our me
his it her I she him us
he you my we their

After school

Dave forgot **Dave's** coat.

Carrie bought an apple and ate **the apple**.

Carrie asked **Carrie's** mum, "Can **Carrie** have an ice cream?"

Mel got **Mel's** football then **Mel** went out to play.

Dave's teacher told **Dave** that **Dave** had forgotten **Dave's** coat.

Mel told Carrie, "**Carrie** can borrow **Mel's** pencil."

Joe and Rose asked **Joe and Rose's** mum, "Can **Joe and Rose** play outside?"

Joe and Rose told Carrie, "**Carrie** can play with **Joe and Rose** at

Joe and Rose's house."

Rose stood on **Rose's** head and said, "Look at **Rose**."

Frank called for Joe and Rose and **Frank** asked **Joe and Rose** if

Joe and Rose wanted to play at **Frank's** house.

Pronouns take their place

Objective

To choose pronouns appropriately.

Background knowledge

Pronouns are often used to make sentences more readable. A sentence like *Leah rode Leah's bike to Leah's house* is an oddity. The form *Leah rode her bike to her house* feels easier to say because it avoids repetition, and makes the text feel more cohesive and coherent. Reading a passage to the class with no pronouns can illustrate this very effectively (it is usually necessary to read a text like this as our brains are used to adding the pronouns automatically!). It is also a good way of identifying when pronouns are needed.

Activities

- **Photocopiable page 21 'Change the sentence'**
As children substitute pronouns for noun phrases the results will vary. A sentence like *Don't eat the cakes* could be changed to *Don't eat them* or *Don't eat those*. It may be interesting to look at the pronoun children use for *My best friend*… Will they use 'he' or 'she'? What guided their choice?
- **Photocopiable page 22 'Missing pronouns'**
This missing-word activity encourages reflection on how pronouns link to other words. To find the appropriate word the children will need to consider what the pronouns actually refer to.
- **Photocopiable page 23 'Choose the pronoun'**
As the children consider their options for the pronoun they could select for the sentences, there will be discussion. Some of the children may have encountered younger children who would say *Me went to the beach*. In certain dialects 'us teacher' as opposed to 'our teacher' could be used. The various possibilities can provide some insights into the varied uses of pronouns and their commonly accepted usage.

Further ideas

- **Pronoun links:** Children could look for pronouns in a text, such as a newspaper article, and circle examples, if possible considering which noun they might represent. They could then try to find and circle the nouns in the same text link the nouns to the pronouns.
- **Which pronoun?:** Note that you may need to present some new terms before attempting this activity. Either using the same texts as the previous idea or new ones, challenge the children to find pronouns and identify them – are they first person, possessive and so on? – to introduce variations, such as 'he', 'him', 'hers'.

Digital content

On the digital component you will find:
- Printable versions of all three photocopiable pages.
- Answers to 'Change the sentence', 'Missing pronouns' and 'Choose the pronoun'.
- Interactive versions of 'Change the sentence' and 'Choose the pronoun'.

Name:

Change the sentence

Pronouns can replace single words or groups of words. Look at this example:

I saw **the little boy** fall off his skateboard.

We can change this using a pronoun:

I saw **him** fall off his skateboard.

'Him' is a pronoun. It replaces 'the little boy'.

■ Look at these sentences. Find one pronoun in the word box that can replace the phrase in bold, and then rewrite the sentence on the line below.

■ After you have finished the sentences, list the pronouns you used and the phrases they replaced. Write them on a separate piece of paper.

she	it	this	us
these	those	them	
him	her	we	he

1. Julie played on **her new roller skates**.

2. Don't eat **the cakes**.

3. Did you find **the lost key**?

4. The teacher told **Leila and me** we could use **the cricket bat**.

5. The boy gave **his little sister** a sweet.

6. Mum couldn't get **the television** to work.

7. **Shaun** said **Josh and I** could have a go on **his bike**.

8. **My best friend** can do a magic trick.

■ Can you think of any new sentences that have words or phrases that could be replaced by pronouns? Write them on a separate sheet of paper.

Name:

Pronouns take their place

Missing pronouns

■ Look at the gaps in the sentences below. Find a word below that fits in each gap.

hers mine we
you yourself him they
I us she he our it
they herself them yours

The animals were at a party. ________________ were bored. Monkey wanted to cheer ________________ up. She found a tree stump and jumped on ________________.

She shouted to the animals "Hey ________________ lot – look at me." She did a funny dance. ________________ bopped and jived. The animals laughed so loudly ________________ gave themselves tummy aches. The camel was not pleased. ________________ was so jealous.

When the monkey was finished he clambered onto the tree stump. "If she can do it so can ________________," he thought. He did a dance. "I bet ________________ is better than ________________," he said to ________________.

The animals thought camel was awful. They shouted "________________ is rubbish. What do you take ________________ for? ________________ don't want any old dancing. Bring back ________________ friend the monkey." They sent ________________ packing.

Choose the pronoun

■ Look at the sentences below. There is a choice of pronouns to complete each sentence.

■ Rewrite the sentences, choosing the correct pronoun for each sentence. Some have two choices.

Give the torch to my. / me. / I. ____________________

Yesterday my / I / me went to the beach. ____________________

He / Him / His played on the swing. ____________________

This is our / we / us house. ____________________

We want us / our / we playtime. ____________________

I blew my / our / mine nose. ____________________

He whistled to he. / himself. / herself. ____________________

Our teacher lost he / him / his keys. ____________________

My mum let me help her / she / I cook the tea. ____________________

Today me / I / our gran is coming to visit. ____________________

We / Us / Our teacher told we / us / our off. ____________________

This / These / Those book is me. / I. / mine. ____________________

Pronouns in text

Objective

To investigate the use of pronouns.

Background knowledge

Pronouns can be ambiguous words. For example, imagine that a note sent by a member of the public to the local council read: *Our kitchen floor is very damp. We have two children and would like a third. Could you please send someone round to do something about it?* That final 'it' is full of ambiguity as it can be taken to refer to the first or the second sentence. Competent writers make good use of this ambiguity, especially in humour and poetry. Most children will find this subtlety difficult to use in their own writing, but they might appreciate jokes that use such ambiguity appropriately. In particular, pronouns that refer to inanimate objects ('it', 'them' and so on) can provide an interesting focus as they can often represent more possibilities than personal pronouns.

Activities

- **Photocopiable page 25 'Pronouns at play'**
This reading activity may be used in shared or guided reading. Children could spend time developing a dramatic delivery of the script in small groups, using the pointing technique for identifying pronouns as outlined on page 16 (notes for photocopiable page 17 'Who is you?').
- **Photocopiable page 26 'Comic pronouns'**
As with many comic stories, the children will find as they read this text that an understanding of the pronouns depends on an appreciation of who and what they are referring to. In some cases this will rely on the picture rather than the text, for example 'they' in *They all look scruffy* is only understood through reference to the illustration.
- **Photocopiable page 27 'Pronoun talk'**
As the children record and investigate their use of pronouns they can compare their findings with others in the class. They could also swap recordings and listen to the conversations others have recorded.

Further ideas

- **Poetry:** Some poems, such as Thomas Hardy's 'Waiting Both', or Walter de la Mare's 'The Listeners' feature consciously ambiguous uses of pronouns. Children could try their own examples. In particular, poets often use this device to highlight uncertainty and strangeness. Although this is difficult for children to emulate in their writing, discussing such work can yield very interesting ideas and speculations.
- **Eerie openings:** Stories often use pronouns to provide an eerie opening, for example, *He was late. He ran through the streets. What if they got there before him?* Children could try creating their own mysterious story openings in the same vein.

Digital content

On the digital component you will find:
- Printable versions of all three photocopiable pages.
- Answers to 'Pronouns at play' and 'Comic pronouns'.

Pronouns in text

Pronouns at play

■ Act out this play with some friends.

■ Look at some of the pronouns in the play. Read the play again. Each time you come to a pronoun, stop and point to the character it refers to.

The Tortoise and the Hare

Cast:
Fox, Hare, Tortoise

Fox: This is a story of two animals and how they decided who was the fastest.

(Hare is sitting with Fox. Tortoise comes past.)

Hare: Hello Tortoise.

Tortoise: Hello Hare. Hello Fox.

Hare: Oh dear, you are so slow.

Tortoise: Am I?

Hare: She is, isn't she, Fox?

Fox: Leave her alone, Hare.

Tortoise: OK, why don't we have a race? The winner will get a medal.

Hare: A race! With you! Ha! I will easily win.

Tortoise: We shall see. Fox, could you start us off?

Fox: Alright. Are you ready? Steady? Go!

(Hare runs far into the lead.)

Hare: Look at me go. The medal will be mine!

Fox: Hurry up Tortoise. Oh dear, she is sure to lose.

Tortoise: Don't worry about me. I know what I'm doing.

(Hare is well in the lead.)

Hare: Where is she? I can't even see her. I think I'll have a rest.

(Falls asleep. Tortoise comes past.)

Tortoise: Just as I thought. He is fast asleep. Shhh, don't want to wake him.

(Fox stands at the finishing line.)

Fox: Come on Tortoise. This is your chance to win.

(Hare wakes up. Sees Tortoise crossing line.)

Hare: She beat me!

Name:

Pronouns in text

Comic pronouns

■ Read this story. Find the pronouns and circle them.

■ Look back at the pronouns. Which person or thing did they refer to?

Name:

Pronoun talk

■ Record a five-minute conversation with two friends on this subject: 'Things people do at playtime'.

■ Listen to the recording. Write down some of the pronouns you used in the discussion in the speech box. In the tag alongside, record what or whom the pronouns referred to.

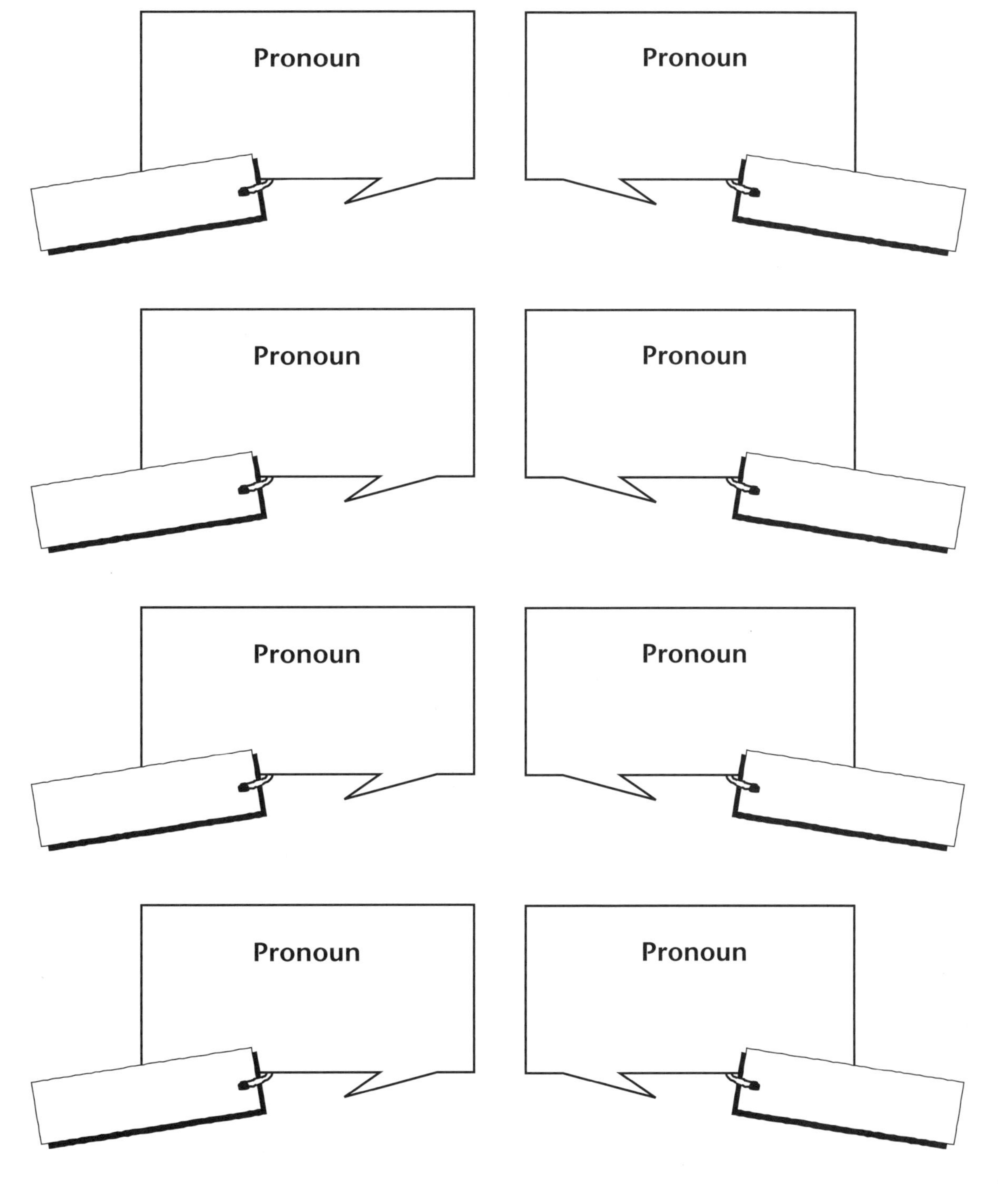

Pronouns in writing

Objective

To extend the use of pronouns in writing.

Writing focus

Building on previous activities on noun and pronouns, this section encourages children to think about using pronouns accurately and effectively in their writing.

Skills to writing

- **Meet the family**

The pronoun family isn't the biggest of crowds (many of them being represented on poster page 10 'Pronouns') but children's accurate grasp of their use and spelling provides a vital toolkit for writing. During shared reading and writing, stop occasionally to check a pronoun and look at what type it is and what it refers to.

- **Reference**

A feature of pronoun use to explore with the children in their writing is the clarity of reference. The activities in this chapter will present a few examples of sentences where it isn't crystal clear what the pronouns are referring to. If children write 'he saw it', encourage them to check that their reader will know who 'he' was and what 'it' is.

- **Playscripts and drama**

As was demonstrated on photocopiable page 25 'Pronouns at play', the use of pronouns in playscripts and drama provides an interesting opportunity to check that the reader and user of the script is clear about what is being referred to. During drama activities, children can think of lines and instances where it needs to be clear who is referring to what. If, in a piece of drama, someone is saying 'bring it to me', they can explore what 'it' is.

- **Person and text type**

It is important to work on person with the children to ensure the consistency of their writing. It is not uncommon for children to switch person halfway through a piece of work. A good way of doing this is to explore some of the text types that children are asked to write. A personal recount, such as a diary entry, will use the first person. A report text will be written in the third person. Persuasive texts can be written in the second person (*You should recycle newspaper because…*).

Activities

- **Photocopiable page 30 'Autobiography planner'**

As part of their work on the first person, children could devise a recount text that consists of their first-person memories. Using the planner, ask them to construct a set of ideas for a recount of their own life story. When they are writing this, encourage them to think of their own 'I' and 'we' memories, and also to look at the involvement of other people in their experiences – 'he', 'she' and 'they'.

- **Photocopiable page 31 'She did what?'**

Before cutting up the grid, look across the columns and find the potential for stories, discussing the implications with the class. For example, *He found it*, is different from *He found her*. To work with this activity, children need to cut out the words on the photocopiable sheet and arrange them on the table. Working in twos, they shuffle the words around, looking at some of the mini-stories or story events they create by putting three words together, such as *I saw it*, and then asking questions such as: *What might I have seen? Why was it so important?*

Write on

- **The... climbed**

Provide the children with a range of sentences where the noun is missing. Ask them to look at the sentence and see if they can come up with a range of possible words to fill the gap. If, for example, the sentence is *The … climbed the tree*, the missing word could be feasible ('girl', 'koala') or more outlandish ('alien', 'teacher').

- **Nonsense nouns**

Nonsense noun poems can be a great way of generating play with word sounds. Challenge the children to write an expressive poem about a strange made-up noun, adding in new nouns as they go along: *The scrumbly has got long dleeeps and a glibble made of splee*. They should keep all verbs and adjectives conventional. Of course, the great thing about nonsense words is that they are so easy to rhyme. That's where 'Jabberwocky' came from!

- **'It' bit more**

When revising writing, ask the children to try a pronoun addition on some of the sentences they have already written. This can provide a way of extending writing to provide more feeling or extended detail. For example, if they have written, *The sun shelter is on the playground*, can they think which pronoun they would use for an extra fact? In the sun shelter's case they would use 'it', so they should think of a sentence that starts 'It…' which could add a bit of extra thought or detail to their writing: *The sun shelter is on the playground. It is bright green.*

- **Pronoun sentences**

Encourage the children to try devising sentences with lots of pronouns in them. It doesn't matter what story they are telling – the purpose is to gather an array of pronouns and use them to stretch out the sentence. For example: *He saw me dropping these so he picked them up and gave them to you*. Once they have devised an elongated sentence they like, the children can illustrate it, possibly giving some insight into what the sentence was all about.

- **Comic pronouns**

Ask the children to produce their own comic stories similar to 'Granny Grammar' (see photocopiable page 26 'Comic pronouns'). As they do this, encourage them to use pronouns, as we would in everyday speech – *Catch these! Look at him!* In doing so they need to make sure that it is clear from the illustrations – the way the characters point, move and look – what the pronoun refers to.

- **What is that?**

Provide a selection of second sentences and challenge the children to devise their own first sentences that would fit with them. For example, start with *It is hers.* Can they think of a sentence that could precede this – such as *The rabbit belongs to the girl* or *The girl has a pink rabbit*? They can then explore different ways of shaping sentences to match the subsequent pronoun.

- **Person and text type**

It is important to work on person with the children to ensure the consistency of their writing. It is not uncommon for children to switch person halfway through a piece of work. A good way of doing this is to explore some of the text types that children are asked to write. A personal recount, such as a diary entry, will use the first person. A report text will be written in the third person. Persuasive texts can be written in the second person (*You should recycle newspaper because…*).

Digital content

On the digital component you will find:

- Printable versions of both photocopiable pages.

Name:

Pronouns in writing

Autobiography planner

- Use this planner to make notes and plan a recount of your own life story.
- Remember to think of:
  - the events that will interest the readers
  - the characters who appeared in your story
  - things people said at the time.

Pronouns in writing

She did what?

■ Using the words below, can you make mini-stories one sentence long? For example: *He found her*. What could the story be about? What ideas does it give for longer story writing?

I	me
he	him
she	her
it	them
they	it
lost	made
found	saw

Chapter 2

Words at work

Introduction

The focus of this chapter is to improve children's understanding of words. It begins by reviewing and developing their knowledge of the main word classes that they will have encountered and then looks at how prefixes can be used to create nouns. The meaning and correct use of indefinite articles is followed by a more investigative approach to understanding the concept of word families. The final section provides support in writing about technical terms, concluding with a range of ideas to help consolidate new knowledge and skills in children's everyday writing. For further practice, please see the 'Words at work' section of the Year 3 workbook.

In this chapter

Word classes page 35	To revise nouns and adjectives, verbs and adverbs.
Forming nouns page 39	To form nouns using a range of prefixes.
Indefinite articles page 43	To use 'a' and 'an' accurately.
Word families page 47	To explore how words can be related in form and meaning.
Wordsmiths page 51	To develop the use of new knowledge and vocabulary.

Poster notes

Prefixes (page 33)

This poster features a selection of words made using prefixes, with each prefix in bold. Use the poster to exemplify the meaning of prefixes and in particular how they can form nouns (they can, of course, form other words too). If appropriate, display the poster and add new words containing prefixes as they arise.

Word families (page 34)

The concepts of word families are explained through two examples: the root words 'run' and 'watch', with other words (sometimes of different classes) that derive from these words placed around each one. It is very important to ensure that everyone understands the meaning of 'word family' in this context.

Vocabulary

Children should already know:

noun, adjective, verb, adverb, suffix

In Year 3 children need to know:

prefix, article (definite and indefinite), word family, consonant, consonant letter, vowel, vowel letter

Words at work
Prefixes
forehead
unhappy
nonsense
disagree
antifreeze
overlook
impossible
superstar
mistake
prefix
telescope

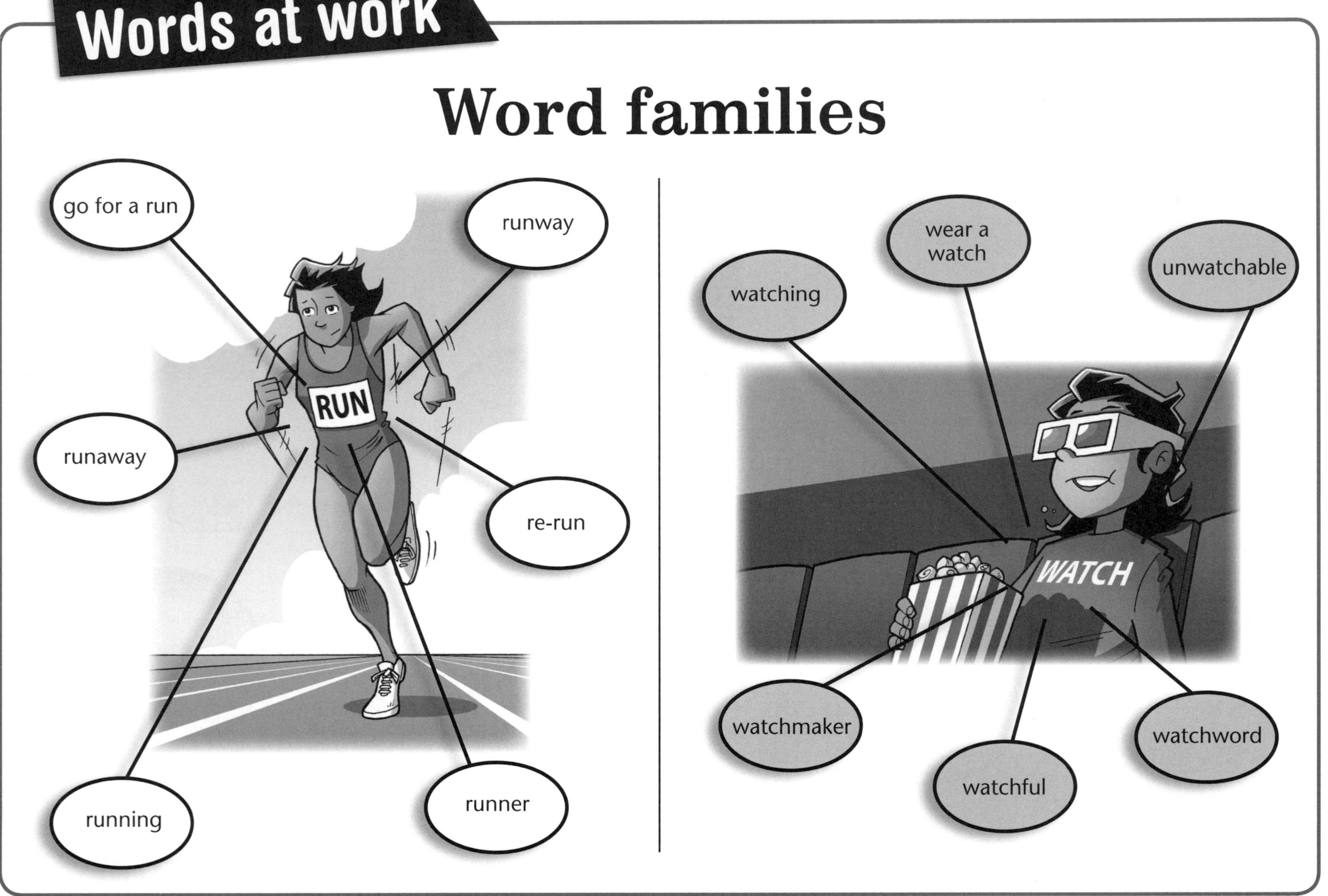

Words at work
Word families
go for a run
runway
RUN
runaway
re-run
running
runner
wear a watch
watching
unwatchable
WATCH
watchmaker
watchword
watchful

Word classes

Objective

To revise nouns and adjectives, verbs and adverbs.

Background knowledge

Although children should have encountered nouns, adjectives, verbs and adverbs before, they may not necessarily be familiar with defining them as 'word classes'. Although there are several other word classes, the four in focus are essential and interdependent in constructing meaningful sentences. Before starting any activities, recap the meaning of each word class and present examples, in particular showing how adjectives relate to nouns and adverbs to verbs, noting spelling patterns as appropriate (for example 'happy', 'happily'). You may find it appropriate to refer to the second poster, 'Word families' (page 34) and consider words that are both nouns and verbs, such as 'watch' and 'run'. (Pages 36–38 present activities to develop understanding of word classes as words linked by form and meaning such as 'foot' and 'football', and not simply letter pattern such as 'ball' and 'wall'.)

Activities

- **Photocopiable page 36 'Nouns and adjectives'**
This activity revises the concept that adjectives describe nouns, helping to consolidate children's understanding of both word classes and their relationship. Work done using these words can be extended by looking for opposites for the adjectives (using the same or different nouns), further emphasising the role of adjectives in setting tone and mood.
- **Photocopiable page 37 'Verbs and adverbs'**
If children have not covered adverbs before, this activity will need to be discussed beforehand. When teaching children how adverbs work, any sentence creation is perhaps best done orally. Note that many of the adverbs shown are only logical for one, perhaps two, of the verbs listed. Creating and listing sentences as a class can allow you to model how different adverbs can be used to enliven writing.
- **Photocopiable page 38 'Identifying word classes'**
This activity helps to consolidate children's understanding of the four word classes encountered in the previous activities. Before attempting this activity ensure that children understand the concept of a colour-coded key, and work with the class to colour code a sample sentence of your own on the board, modelling how to identify the four different word classes in focus. If you want to include other classes, such as pronouns, this should be easy to accommodate in this activity or in your own sentences.

Further ideas

- **Opposites:** Repeat the activities on pages 36 and 37, but change every adjective and adverb to its opposite before starting.
- **Considering texts:** Present children with photocopies of suitable texts (or display them on your whiteboard) and identify further examples of each word class.
- **Word swapping:** Focus in on particular sentences (either from the activities presented on pages 36 to 38, or from selected texts) and consider how the meaning might be changed by altering certain words from one of the four classes considered.

Digital content

On the digital component you will find:

- Printable versions of all three photocopiable pages.
- Answers to 'Identifying word classes'.

Name:

Word classes

Nouns and adjectives

The main job of a noun is to name things such as 'dog' or 'house'. Adjectives help us to describe what these things are like, such as 'black dog' or 'old house'. Sometimes we can use more than one adjective with a noun, such as 'the large, old house'.

- Use any of these adjectives with nouns to make some sentences. Can you make any sentences with two adjectives?

Adjectives

round red lazy hot
awful happy wet
green broken clever
old angry cold

Nouns

boy wolf hat paint
light fence coat
pencil teacher meal
girl cat pond

1. *The lazy boy went to bed.*
2. __________
3. __________
4. __________
5. __________
6. __________
7. __________
8. __________

Word classes

Verbs and adverbs

Verbs are often doing words, such as 'run' or 'eat'. Adverbs describe how these things are done, such as 'run quickly' or 'eat slowly'.

■ Draw a line to match each verb to an adverb that you think goes well with it. Discuss your ideas with a partner. Try to put them into sentences, such as: *You must think carefully if you want to get the correct answer.*

Verbs	**Adverbs**
run	quietly
write	carefully
play	quickly
eat	nicely
think	happily
sing	neatly
watch	angrily
talk	slowly
type	noisily
shout	merrily

Name:

Word classes

Identifying word classes

■ Choose a colour for each word class and shade the key, then shade any nouns, verbs, adjectives and adverbs in the sentences below using the correct colour to match the key.

Key	
Word class	**Colour**
Adjective	
Adverb	
Noun	
Verb	

1. The furry dog ate all the food.
2. She ran quickly down the wide street.
3. She dived gracefully into the clear, blue water.
4. She leaped carelessly into the crisp, white snow.
5. You should eat lots of fruit and vegetables every day.
6. The baby screamed noisily because he wanted a drink.
7. The yellow bus stopped suddenly at the busy crossing.
8. He hit the ball so hard that it landed outside the playground.
9. He watched nervously as the dark, thick snake slithered slowly towards him.
10. The class waited quietly until the bell rang, and then walked to the playground.

Forming nouns

Objective

To form nouns using a range of prefixes.

Background knowledge

Although the curriculum focus requires children to use prefixes to form new nouns, the majority of words formed with prefixes are adjectives, adverbs and verbs. As such, it is important to carefully introduce children to the concept of prefixes – they are groups of letters that are not usually words in their own right, but do have a meaning (for example, 'un' means 'not'). Remember also that there are many prefixes, but a small number ('dis', 'in', 're', 'un') account for most everyday uses of prefixes, and most of those (except 're') mean 'not'!

Note also that some prefixes require a hyphen, although no prefix alters the spelling of the word it attaches to. At this stage the main thing to note is that children need not consider rules as to how any word takes a particular prefix, and that many word classes use prefixes.

Activities

- **Photocopiable page 40 'Prefix meanings'**

This page introduces and develops understanding of the meaning of different prefixes. If the children know the target words they will probably be able to deduce the meanings; if not, a dictionary may be required. Note that these words are also on the poster provided on page 33. This work can easily be extended by investigating appropriate texts.

- **Photocopiable page 41 'It's NOT fair!'**

This activity broadens understanding that different prefixes can have the same meaning (in this case 'not'). Knowing which words take which prefix is a matter of familiarity, not rules, and you should be aware in developing work on prefixes that younger children often struggle to think of new examples. Once children have worked through the sheet, spend time looking at the words that use 'not' prefixes and consider their meanings without the prefix.

- **Photocopiable page 42 'New nouns'**

Children have to identify nouns that have been formed using prefixes, then take these prefixes and use them to form a new noun and use it in a sentence. In developing this work further, you should be aware that it is tricky to find suitable nouns that use prefixes for this age group. More confident learners could be challenged to investigate the origin and meaning of the prefix using appropriate reference books.

Further ideas

- **Prefix wall:** Create a display showing words that use prefixes. For each one, clearly show the prefix and the root word, identifying the meaning of the prefix and the word class. Allow children to add to this as they encounter new words, encouraging them to spend a few minutes scanning their texts after reading to identify such words.
- **Suffixes too!:** If the class is already familiar with suffixes, recap these, looking at words that are made with both prefixes and suffixes (for example 'un-eat-able', 'inter-act-ion', 'ir-respons-ible'). Note that prefixes do not change the spelling of the word they attach to, but suffixes sometimes do.

Digital content

On the digital component you will find:

- Printable versions of all three photocopiable pages.
- Answers to all three photocopiable pages.
- Interactive version of 'It's NOT fair!'.

Name:

Forming nouns

Prefix meanings

■ Look at these words made using prefixes, then write down the information for each one. One has already been done for you.

~~prefix~~ forehead impossible mistake nonsense
disagree subway superpower telescope unhappy

word	prefix
prefix	pre
meaning	before

word	
prefix	
meaning	

word	
prefix	
meaning	

word	
prefix	
meaning	

word	
prefix	
meaning	

word	
prefix	
meaning	

word	
prefix	
meaning	

word	
prefix	
meaning	

word	
prefix	
meaning	

word	
prefix	
meaning	

Forming nouns

It's NOT fair!

■ There are lots of different prefixes, and to make things even harder, some of them have the same meaning. Can you find all the prefixes that mean 'not' in the passage below? Which prefix is used the most?

dis   il   im   in   non   un

Tim's boat

Tim had spent ages making his boat. He had even painted the inside of it. It was very uncomfortable bending over for hours on end painting all those bits of card and string. Finally, although he knew it was imperfect, Tim decided that it was finished and that he wanted to sail it on the sea. Tim's dad thought the idea was nonsense. "It's illogical!" he said. "All that effort! It won't come back you know."

"Oh leave him alone," said Mum. "His ideas might be incorrect and you might disagree, but it's his boat and he wants to do it."

And so the day came. Tim placed it on the water's edge and the boat moved non-stop until it was far from the shore. Soon, the uneven waves turned the boat onto its side and it began to sink, before disappearing beneath the waves. Little Tim's sadness was indescribable: he cried, he screamed, he tried to run into the sea, but to rescue the boat was impossible. After a while they went home. Tim felt very unhappy, and that night his supper was discarded and remained uneaten. As for the toy boat, it sank slowly to the sea bed where it remained, undisturbed and undiscovered, as the sand slowly covered it.

Name:

Forming nouns

New nouns

■ Each of the five sentences below contains a noun that has been made by adding a prefix to a word. Underline each one, and then use the prefixes to make five new nouns and put them each in a sentence. (There are some nouns at the bottom of the page to help you.)

1. The finger next to your thumb is called your forefinger.

2. To get to the other side of the road safely you should use the subway.

3. The car was parked at the top of the multistorey car park.

4. She spoke to her friend on the telephone.

5. He wrote an autobiography to tell everyone about his life.

marine scope car media head

Indefinite articles

Objective

To use 'a' and 'an' accurately.

Background knowledge

Although the focus of this unit is the indefinite articles 'a' and 'an', the unit also introduces the definite article, 'the'. Children at this stage are usually quite able to appreciate the difference between the specific and non-specific nature of the articles. Ideally the children should be able to apply the 'article' test to a word to see if it is a noun – can it accept, 'a', 'an' or 'the' and still make sense? You may need to revisit some phonic work to explain why words beginning in 'h' may require 'an' while words beginning in a vowel may not. The rules are relatively simple and concern sounds:

Letter and sound	Example	Indefinite article
Consonant letter with consonant sound	dog	a
Consonant letter with vowel sound	hour	an
Vowel letter with vowel sound	ear	an
Vowel letter with consonant sound	one-liner	a

Also important is the role of adjectives in affecting indirect articles. So, 'a bus' that is old would become 'an old bus' as the vowel sound of 'old' is the first sound after the article.

Activities

- **Photocopiable page 44 'Nouns sort'**

In this activity, the children are required to group nouns according to whether they would take 'a' or 'an'. There is also a selection of non-nouns to keep them on their toes! Prepare the class for this activity by running through the rules outlined above, modelling and reinforcing the terminology as appropriate. There are many words in the activity that provide scope for reinforcing the rules.

- **Photocopiable page 45 'Know your articles'**

This activity introduces the definite article 'the' and will help the children to understand the difference between it and indefinite articles.

- **Photocopiable page 46 'A or an?'**

This activity provides further reinforcement by considering indefinite articles in context. Remind the children that it is the sound after the article that decides what it should be, emphasising that the main reason for using 'an' is to make speech flow more smoothly – having two vowels next to each other forces the speaker to break their flow. Reading the completed text to the class should emphasise this, especially if it is read initially using 'a' in every place where 'an' is required.

Further ideas

- **Lose the ans!:** Present children with a text that contains lots of 'an's, and explain that their mission is to change them all to 'a's by inserting appropriate adjectives. The opposite can also be attempted but it is harder. (The activity on page 45 could work for this. Simply ask children to reverse each article and alter subsequent words appropriately.)
- **Phonics revisited:** Make a list of all vowel sounds, and their graphemes, that might be preceded by 'an'. Display these in the classroom and add wordbanks beneath them.

Digital content

On the digital component you will find:

- Printable versions of all three photocopiable pages.
- Answers to all three photocopiable pages.
- Interactive version of 'Nouns sort'.

Name:

Indefinite articles

Nouns sort

■ Look at the words below and decide which ones are nouns, then put them in the correct set. Will they have 'a' or 'an'? Words that are not nouns should be written outside the sets.

A

An

ball	apple	pencil	eat	orange	honour
walking	watch	eye	hour	unicorn	house
hoe	unicycle	X-ray	hotel	because	iceberg

Indefinite articles

Know your articles

The words 'a', 'an' and 'the' are called articles. They are used before nouns.

'The' is a definite article: it is used to refer to a particular thing. For example, if someone says, *Put it on the table,* the listener should know which table the speaker is referring to.

'A' and 'an' are indefinite articles. They are used when speaking about something in general terms. For example, *Put it on a table*, could be any table.

■ Look at each of the sentences below and circle the articles in each one, stating if they are definite or indefinite. The first one has been done for you.

1. I am going to the shop to buy an orange and a loaf of bread.

2. The class computer was broken so she had to use a pen and paper.

3. She looked out of the window and saw a small boy approaching.

4. I'd like an apple, a banana and a glass of water please.

5. The dog wanted to go outside. It thought there was a cat in the garden.

6. I ran to the station but I missed the 9pm train. I had to catch a different one.

Name:

Indefinite articles

A or an?

■ Read the passage below and insert the correct indirect article ('a' or 'an') in each space. Read your work aloud to help you decide if you are correct.

A small tail

There was ______ long, winding road that went to ______ old house. Some people said that it was ______ haunted house, and that ______ ghost had been seen there many times. One day ______ young boy approached the house. He was wearing ______ onesie that was red with green spots on, and his face was as round as ______ orange. He picked up ______ heavy stone and threw it at the front door, which opened with ______ eerie creak as soon as the stone hit it. ______ elderly woman appeared and gave ______ friendly smile, but the boy stepped back in fear as he noticed ______ old dog standing next to the woman. He looked closely and saw that it was ______ one-eyed dog. In fact, it was ______ huge, old, one-eyed dog! The dog wagged its small tail and gave ______ happy bark but it was too late, he was already running away, as fast as his little legs could carry him.

Word families

Objective

To understand how words can be related in form and meaning.

Background knowledge

Often in the infant years word families are presented as words that share letter patterns, such as 'ball' and 'wall'. While this is entirely appropriate and helpful when presented as part of a phonics or spelling programme, it is not how grammarians view the term 'word family'. By this age children should start to be made aware that all words have origins, and that root words often form the basis of many other words, their family. This is also a useful method for building vocabulary quickly.

While children do not need to encounter terms such as 'etymology' (why and how words mean what they do, their origins), and 'morphology' (how words are created using roots, prefixes, suffixes and other roots), their awareness of how their language is constructed should begin to grow through exposure to appropriate vocabulary in discrete and meaningful contexts.

Activities

- **Photocopiable page 48 'Compound words'**

To help secure the foundations for children's understanding of morphology and word families, this activity recaps and develops compound words. Although it is not necessary to go into too much depth, it is worth children seeing that a compound word is the bringing together of two root words, and in some cases these form a single word, sometimes a hyphenated word, and even two separate words that nevertheless are considered to have a single meaning, such as 'running shoe'.

- **Photocopiable page 49 'Do and doer'**

This activity helps the children to see how different word classes can belong to the same family of words. Using picture clues they must write the noun that defines a person taking part in a particular action – for example 'runner' – and the verb that relates to this word, in this case 'to run'. Note that the next activity will take these concepts further, but for the moment it is enough to ensure that the children grasp the connection between roots and families. (Note that 'sailor' is the odd word out spelling-wise.)

- **Photocopiable page 50 'Root and branch'**

This activity is best introduced with reference to the poster on page 34. Ideally display this poster as large as possible on your whiteboard and discuss each word family in turn, focusing on word classes and how each word in the family has been formed. In particular point out that both the words 'watch' and 'run' in their root form are both verb and noun. For the activity itself, guide the children to choosing root words wisely, perhaps pointing them to some of the pictures from the previous exercise, some of which provide wide-ranging word families.

Further ideas

- **The whole family:** Using an identified word family (such as from the poster page 34), challenge the children to write a paragraph that includes one instance of each word in the family.
- **Get classy:** Develop the 'root and branch' activity further by challenging children to write the class of each word in the family. More confident learners could be challenged to identify how each word has been made (for example with the suffix 'ing' added), and if appropriate, research the meaning and origin of the root word.

Digital content

On the digital component you will find:

- Printable versions of all three photocopiable pages.
- Answers to 'Compound words' and 'Do and doer'.
- Interactive version of 'Compound words'.

Name:

Word families

Compound words

■ Join each word on the left to its partner on the right to form eight compound words. Write the words in the box opposite. (You might use a dictionary to help you decide if you need a hyphen or a space between them.) One has been done for you.

post	pin
table	board
light	card
straw	cloth
screw	ache
safety	paper
white	berry
tooth	house
dust	bin
news	driver

1. postcard
2.
3.
4.
5.
6.
7.
8.
9.
10.

■ Here are 20 root words in alphabetical order. Can you put them in pairs to find ten compound words? Write them in the box opposite. One has been done for you.

ball, ~~boy~~, butter, ~~cow,~~ cuffs, fly, foot, foot, hand, head, home, lamp, path, proof, some, table, time, water, where, work

1. cowboy
2.
3.
4.
5.
6.
7.
8.
9.
10.

Word families

Do and doer

■ Nouns and verbs are often connected to each other: they belong to the same family. For each of the pictures below write the correct noun and verb. The first one has been done for you.

Noun	**Verb**
runner	to run
walker	
swimmer	
writer	
reader	
sailor	
driver	
teacher	
gardener	
skater	

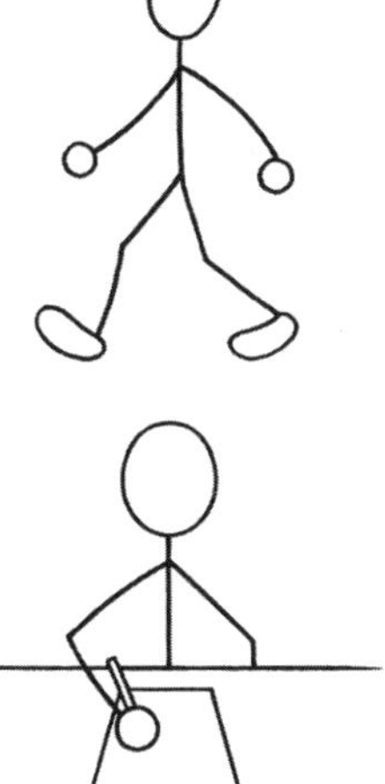

 Name:

Word families

Root and branch

■ Choose two different root words, find as many words in its family as you can then complete the word trees below. A dictionary might help you with words that have the root at the start, but think carefully about words that have used a prefix.

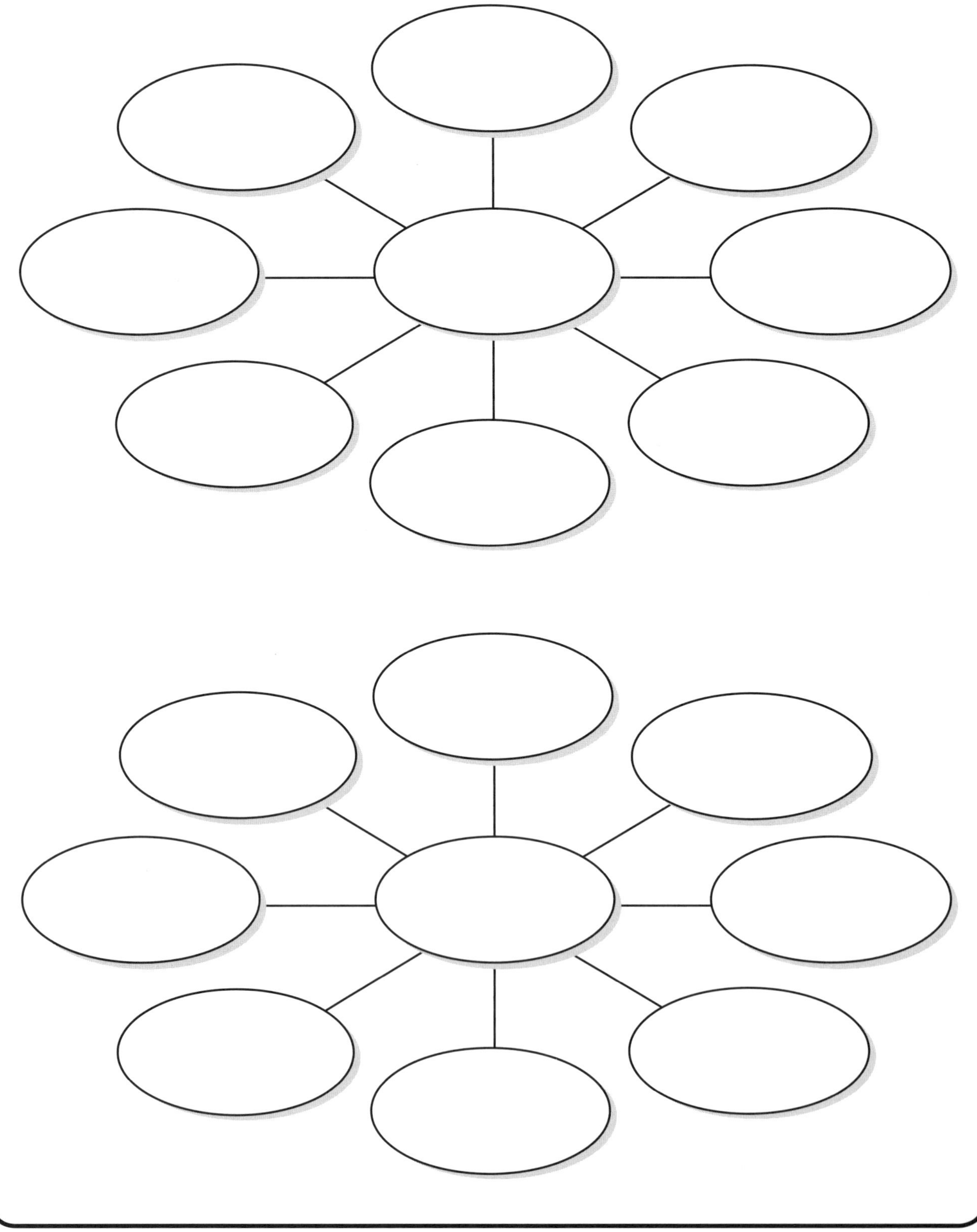

Wordsmiths

Objective

To develop the use of new knowledge and vocabulary.

Writing focus

The focus of this chapter has been very much at word level, covering a range of grammatical concepts and terms. To conclude it, this writing section provides ideas for activities to consolidate each aspect covered – word classes, prefixes, articles and word families, and the two photocopiable sheets recap and consolidate this work, encouraging the children to use technical vocabulary and access dictionaries as desired. The 'Write on' section provides ideas for how teachers can encourage children to use this knowledge to improve their writing.

Skills to writing

- **Be aware**

Providing children with a good range of modelled texts is part of every teacher's work, but analysing the content of these texts can be a good final activity once aspects such as comprehension have been covered. This can lead to fundamental queries such as: *Do newspaper reports have as many adjectives as poems? Are there differences in the range of nouns and verbs used in fiction or non-fiction texts?* If time permits, raising awareness of this can help inform children's subsequent writing with appropriate word lists and checklists. Obviously this approach can extend to other word types and the use of articles.

- **Build vocabulary**

It is all very well learning about word families, prefixes and so on, but the vital thing in all of this is that children's vocabulary grows. This only happens if they encounter and use new vocabulary in both regular and meaningful contexts. In all classroom work, whether looking at grammar, literature or in children's own creative work, it is essential that they are given opportunities to experience and access a wide and growing bank of vocabulary. Displays can help with this, as can teachers modelling words discretely and in context, provide sessions for children to focus. It is helpful to only on improving the vocabulary in their work (and this need not necessarily include spelling). Children also need opportunities to use these words in spoken contexts – at the very least reading them aloud.

Activities

- **Photocopiable page 53 'Understanding words'**

This photocopiable sheet provides an example and structured frames to help develop children's understanding of the more technical aspect of word relationships. After an example based on the poster on page 34, the children are asked to repeat this for two further words, and each time the number of related words required is increased. Teachers may need to prompt with ideas, although the previous sections provide many possibilities. As in previous sections of this chapter, asking the children to produce sentences with the focus word families in can be a useful consolidation.

- **Photocopiable page 54 'Getting technical'**

This activity is intended to recap all of the technical grammatical terms encountered in the chapter. Although it may appear rather dry, it serves as a useful reinforcement. Children who might struggle with this could complete it with written support or using cue cards. Creating a larger version of this for display/ reference may be useful, as would providing a blank template that children can add new terms to as they arise.

Write on

- **Which class are you in?**

For this activity you will need to prepare a text on-screen. You will need a simple piece of writing that has six to ten sentences, either individual or forming a whole. Ideally every sentence should have one each of a noun, adjective, verb and adverb in it. Make four separate versions of the text. In version one remove all the nouns, in two remove the adjectives, and so on, labelling each text clearly, for example: 'Version 1 – word class missing: adverbs'. Distribute the same number of copies of each version so that each child has one text, and ask them to complete the missing words. Next, bring the children together to compare work and decide on their choices, ensuring they use appropriate vocabulary as they do so.

- **Beyond belief**

As already mentioned, asking children to create new nouns (or indeed any words using prefixes) to order and without support is a very difficult task. As such, to reinforce the essential concept that prefixes can be added to existing words to create words with new meaning, choose a focus such as superheroes, robots, magical lands and so on that allows for invented vocabulary. With the context established, provide appropriate prefix lists (for example 'super', 'hyper', 'ultra', 'mega') and ask the children to create new nouns that relate to this context, then move towards sentences, stories or poems (for example *The hyper-palm of the island of Whoohoo produces mega-nuts that weigh as much as a baby elephant!)* If successful this can be taken to another level by creating new and/or onomatopoeic prefixes, such as 'whizz', 'boing', 'woosh' and so on.

- **Before and after**

Writing breaking new reports about (low-level) events or crimes is a good way to reinforce the use of indefinite articles. Simple reports tend to be non-specific because the actual events are unknown or uncertain. For example: *A man is reported to have left a wallet in an ice-cream van on Watson Street today. More news soon...* After creating a bank of such snippets – either teacher- or child-generated – the next activity could be to write a follow-up report where the circumstances have been revealed, thus making it specific and requiring the use of definite articles. For example: *We can report that the wallet lost yesterday in Watson street has been found. The owner, Mr Dimble, had left it on the counter of Mrs Holmes's ice-cream van. Mrs Holmes returned the wallet and to celebrate Mr Dimble bought 99s for everyone.*

- **Meet my family**

Once children are familiar with a selection of word families, a fun and rather more light-hearted activity is to let them invent a root word of their own and create a whole family based around it. They should be encouraged to create words in different classes and to provide meanings for each word. This can link to the imaginary/fantasy work mentioned above relating to prefixes.

Digital content

On the digital component you will find:

- Printable versions of both photocopiable pages.

Wordsmiths

Understanding words

■ Look at the example below. It contains a root word and some of its family, with word class and the meaning given for each word. Choose two other words and repeat this. Your teacher can suggest good root words to choose if you need help.

Root word and family	Class	Meaning
to run	verb	to move quickly
runner	noun	a person who runs as a sport or a hobby
re-run	noun	a repeat of a race or TV series
runaway	compound noun	a person who has run away

Root word and family	Class	Meaning

Root word and family	Class	Meaning

Name:

Wordsmiths

Getting technical

■ It's good to know how our language works. We all use hundreds (or maybe thousands) of words every day, almost without thinking, but there are rules about every word we use. We learn about rules all the time in maths, like the ones for adding and multiplying, so we should really know them for English too. Can you complete this chart?

Technical term	Meaning	Example
Noun	a thing	a table
Verb		
Adverb		
Adjective		
Prefix		
Suffix		
Indirect article		
Direct article		
Word class		
Root word		
Word family		

Chapter 3

Verbs and tenses

Introduction

This chapter looks at some key tenses of verbs and introduces grammatical terms while focusing on an expanding range of verbs for children to incorporate into their work and speech. It also looks at the way verbs are matched to the context in which they are used.

After a gentle introduction reviewing the meaning and use of verbs, subsequent sections move onto grammatical awareness of tenses, including the present perfect, and the effective use of verbs in writing. The concluding writing activities provide opportunities for children to experiment with tenses while strengthening their initial understanding of tenses and forms. For further practice, please see the 'Verbs and tenses' section of the Year 3 workbook.

In this chapter

Reviewing verbs page 58	To recognise and understand the function of verbs in sentences.
Verb tenses page 62	To understand and use verb tenses correctly.
Writing about the past page 66	To understand that there are different ways of writing about events that have already happened.
Tense spotting page 70	To use different verb tenses in writing.
Verbs in writing page 74	To develop the use of verbs and verb tenses in writing.

Poster notes

Alternative verbs (page 56)
As children look at the selection and effect of various verbs, this poster provides a basic thesaurus with which they can select the appropriate term for an action. It can be used as a tool for writing or as a way of spicing up sentences when redrafting, as well as for developing the scope of their vocabulary.

Past, present and future (page 57)
This poster provides examples of the past and present tenses and the future form of some common verbs. It can be displayed as a reminder of how time can be expressed. Boxes or whole columns can be covered, leaving groups to suggest what the missing words could be.

Vocabulary

Children should already know:
verb, adverb, tense (past, present)
In Year 3 children need to know:
present perfect

Verbs and tenses

Alternative verbs

look	say	walk	run	find	hold	jump	make
see	whisper	stroll	dart	discover	grip	bound	assemble
peep	shout	pace	dash	unearth	grasp	spring	create
regard	mumble	step	scarper	disclose	seize	hop	construct
watch	announce	trudge	sprint	acquire	grab	leap	produce
view	speak	shuffle	scramble	recover	clutch	pounce	manufacture
gaze	tell	amble	scurry	spot	possess	bounce	build
gape	remark	move	hurry	learn	clasp	vault	generate
gawk	mention	march	race	notice	squeeze	lurch	fashion

Verbs and tenses

Past, present and future

In the past I	Now I	In the future I
looked	look	will look
said	say	will say
walked	walk	will walk
ran	run	will run
found	find	will find
held	hold	will hold
jumped	jump	will jump
made	make	will make

Reviewing verbs

Objective

To recognise and understand the function of verbs in sentences.

Background knowledge

This section acts as both review and consolidation of children's awareness of verbs, with activities focused on finding and identifying verbs in different contexts, and selecting appropriate verbs to fit the context. Class discussion and exemplification around these activities should be focused on what verbs are ('doing' words) and how to identify them.

Activities

- **Photocopiable page 59 'Verb hunt'**

Children can encounter a range of verbs by looking at different types of text. This activity presents a range of short texts and encourages the children to locate verbs. It is an activity that should naturally motivate the children to point out verbs in their immediate environment, such as those to be found in displays, notices, signs, and so on.

- **Photocopiable page 60 'Change the verb'**

This activity asks children to seek out an alternative verb to cover an action. It is this type of thesaurus-type act of selection that can enrich writing. It also reinforces the reading skill of understanding the type of word that fits a particular context. Through exchanging the verbs in the sentences in this activity children are developing their practical use of this skill.

- **Photocopiable page 61 'Can't without one!'**

Ask the children to look at these sentences, find where they think a verb could be inserted and decide what verb it could be. They can then compare their results. There will probably be a consistent response as to where the verbs should be placed but there may be some variety in the verbs that are selected. This could lead to discussion about the type of verb we usually employ to describe an action. For example, *The girl... a goal* could be *The girl scored a goal* but probably not *The girl made a goal* (although this is entirely feasible) and the subtle differences in meaning between similar verbs.

Further ideas

- **Verb thesaurus:** Ask the children to start individual 'verb thesauruses' in books, or start a class one on a display that new verbs can be added to and categorised in – linking them to verbs with similar meanings and/or similar areas of activity (such as movement, the senses and so on).
- **Synonyms in writing:** In their story writing, children can be encouraged to use synonymous verbs as a way of varying the language they use to describe what characters do, and think, and how they behave.
- **Redrafting:** Children can look at samples of writing they have done in order to focus on the following redrafting activity: ask the children to find a verb they have used. Can they think of two other verbs that could have been placed in that context? Which verb will they select as the best for that context? Can they explain why you chose that verb?

Digital content

On the digital component you will find:

- Printable versions of all three photocopiable pages.
- Answers to all three photocopiable pages.
- Interactive versions of 'Verb hunt' and 'Change the verb'.

Reviewing verbs

Verb hunt

■ Look for the verbs in these sentences. Remember that a verb can be a word or group of words. Draw a circle round any verbs you find.

■ Collect the verbs you have found. Look at someone else's collection. Did you find the same verbs?

■ How many of your verbs can you use in new sentences? On a separate piece of paper, write some sentences with them.

Name:

Reviewing verbs

Change the verb

■ Look at the sentences below. Each of them contains a verb. Cut out the sentences and swap the verb for a juicy verb.

■ Write your new sentence on a separate sheet of paper.

Juicy verbs		
slithered	bounced	shrieked
leaped	giggled	tumbled
dashed	halted	shattered
gobbled		pounced

Sentences		
Everyone	laughed	at the joke.
"Fire! Fire!"	the boy	said.
The snake	went	into the grass.
The window	broke	into many pieces.
The ball	went	down the stairs.
The tiger	came out	of the bushes.
The acrobats	moved	around the circus ring.
We	ran	for safety.
The train	stopped	before the broken bridge.
The frog	went	into the water.
The greedy goblin	ate	all the food.

Reviewing verbs

Can't without one!

■ Each of these sentences has a verb missing. Can you guess what it is and mark where it should go?

The chicken away from the fox.

I my lost keys.

The girl a goal.

The boy into the swimming pool.

The sun shining.

Can you me a story?

A bird up into a tree.

The red monster the green monster.

We pictures of our faces.

The cow the grass.

Yesterday it Tuesday.

The man the car.

■ Can you write your own verbless sentences for your friends to try and solve?

____

____

____

Verb tenses

Objective

To understand and use verb tenses correctly.

Background knowledge

Tense shows the timing of a verb. It is the way a verb changes to show whether an action happened in the present ('I run') or the past ('I ran'). The word alters to denote when something happens. There are two simple tenses:

- **Present tense:** This is used to talk about what is happening now or what habitually happens (for example: *I walk to school every day; I am happy.*)
- **Past tense:** This is used to talk about past events. The common ending for past-tense verbs is 'ed', though many verbs are irregular (for example: *I walked home from school; I swam at the weekend*).
- **Future:** English does not have a discrete future tense. It is made in a compound form using a present tense ('I will', 'I may' and so on) and an infinitive (for example: *I will go to the shops; I may see you tomorrow*).

Different tenses are commonly used in different types of writing. For example, a weather report will set sentences in the future, and a diary will usually record events that have happened in the past.

Activities

- **Photocopiable page 63 'Past, present or future'**

This activity revises the three simple tense forms. Ask the children to cut out the sentences, and then encourage them to say the sentences out loud before sorting them into past, present and future. They may want to make up some cards of their own, recording additional sentences that can be spoken aloud, then placing them in the correct group.

- **Photocopiable page 64 'Using tenses'**

By using verbs in their tenses in this activity, the children can develop their understanding of how the tenses feature in certain types of sentence and the way the form of the verb indicates its tense. As an extra challenge, the children could try including more than one of the verbs shown in a sentence.

- **Photocopiable page 65 'Write start'**

Ask the children to think ahead to the type of writing they will be doing in each of the three sections of the sheet – whether it will need to be written in the past, the present, or the future. It is important that the three examples are written in close proximity to each other, to reinforce differences in the tenses. Follow up by focusing on the reasons children used particular tenses.

Further ideas

- **Spelling:** As the children engage in these activities, they may begin to comment on the spelling patterns evident in the various tenses. These can be highlighted and irregular verbs can also be noted.
- **Role play:** Working in groups of four, ask two children to act out a conversation and the other two to listen to them. The conversation could be about things they enjoy or places they have visited. As they speak, the listeners should make notes of the different tenses used. This will usually lead to the two role-players guiding their talk around the tenses and even pausing while notes are made, providing an insight into the use of tenses at different points in a conversation.
- **Tense ping-pong:** As a way of revisiting tenses ask the children to say sentences that describe what they are doing today beginning with the words 'Today I...' They can then recreate those sentences in the past tense, beginning 'Yesterday I...'. This is a good activity to try with a partner. One child begins the activity with a 'Today I...' sentence which their partner has to remodel beginning 'Yesterday I...'.

Digital content

On the digital component you will find:

- Printable versions of all three photocopiable pages.
- Answers to 'Past, present or future'.
- Interactive version of 'Past, present or future'.

Name:

Verb tenses

Past, present or future

■ Cut out the sentences. Say them aloud, then sort them into three piles.

Sentences that will happen in the future.

I will ask the teacher.	She will write a letter.	I saw my friend.
I think about stories.	You know the answer.	I brought my lunch box.
He writes a note.	I will ride my bike.	I leave the pips.
I heard music.	I found a pencil.	I will see you tomorrow.
You stopped moving.	I change my socks.	They will have their tea.

Name:

Verb tenses

Using tenses

■ Look at these verbs.

run		ran		make
	made		found	
find		says		said

■ Try to write eight sentences, each one containing a different verb chosen from the box above.

1. ______________________________

2. ______________________________

3. ______________________________

4. ______________________________

5. ______________________________

6. ______________________________

7. ______________________________

8. ______________________________

Name:

Verb tenses

Write start

- Write some opening lines for different texts in the boxes below.
- Look at the verbs you have used in each piece of writing. Fill in the grid.

a diary extract about things that happened yesterday at school

a recipe for making toast or a cup of tea

a plan for what you will do in your next school holiday

Type of writing	Tense used
diary	
recipe	
holiday plan	

Writing about the past

Objective

To understand that there are different ways of writing about events that have already happened.

Background knowledge

This section introduces children to words and structures used for speaking and writing about the past. Following on from the previous section, it recaps what is meant by the past tense and how it is formed, before moving on to carefully introducing the 'present perfect' form (*I have walked*, *I have eaten*) while allowing children to distinguish between the meaning and intent of both tenses.

You must be careful to ensure that children do not get muddled, as this can become complicated. Remember that the perfect is formed using the present tense of the verb 'to have' as an auxiliary along with the 'past participle' of the main verb, but also note that this same participle is used for passive statements (*I was seen*) and also the past perfect (*I had walked*). Children may implicitly understand both the perfect and passive forms when encountered in texts but explicit teaching of these forms should be avoided at this stage.

Activities

- **Photocopiable page 67 'Changing tenses'**

There are two useful strategies that you can use when children are remodelling language from one tense to another. Firstly, say the sentence aloud and remodel it in speech before writing it down. Secondly, it helps if the children think of the present-tense sentence as happening 'today' and the past-tense sentence as happening 'yesterday'. These words tend to provide a useful way of focusing the language in the past or present.

- **Photocopiable page 68 'I'm perfect!'**

This activity implicitly introduces children to the concept of the present perfect tense, asking them to identify the verbs written in the first person and rewrite them in the third person. Use this as an opportunity to consolidate children's appreciation of the present perfect by considering how sentences would be written for a boy, and then for more than one person.

- **Photocopiable page 69 'Nag, nag, nag'**

This activity further reinforces the structure of the present perfect in writing. Children will probably have few problems using this in speech, but the positioning of the words in questions and sentences is different and it is important to recognise this. If desired use this opportunity to stress both the relevance of the present perfect – it connects the past to the present – as well as the positioning of words to form a question. Some children may automatically add adverbs – for example, *Have you ever been to London?* – you should respond to this as appropriate.

Further ideas

- **Diary sentences:** Ask children to offer examples of things that they do throughout the school day (such as *We go to assembly, We paint a picture*) and then rephrase these in the past tense, as if they were written in a diary.
- **Servants' orders:** Following on from the 'I'm perfect' and 'Nag, nag, nag' activities, ask the children to imagine they are a servant in a castle of old (or some other scenario if relevant to current topics) and keep a running commentary of their recently completed work.
- **Have you ever?:** Create a display of fantastical questions such as *Have you ever been to the moon?* and have children add equally fantastical answers and further questions.

Digital content

On the digital component you will find:

- Printable versions of all three photocopiable pages.
- Answers to all three photocopiable pages.
- Interactive version of 'Changing tenses'.

Writing about the past

Changing tenses

- Look at these sentences written in the present tense.
- First, underline all the verbs. Then change all the verbs to the past tense and write the sentences again.
- The first sentence has been done for you.

Present tense	Past tense
I run and kick the ball.	I ran and kicked the ball.
You sing and we ask you to stop.	
He wears scruffy shoes and trips over the laces.	
I pour the juice and drink it slowly.	
We make a den, paint a sign and hang it on the door.	
My aunty climbs the ladder and clears the gutter.	
My dad cooks pancakes and tosses them in the air.	
The pilot flies the plane and lands it at the airport.	

Name:

Writing about the past

I'm perfect!

■ Are you as good as the person who has done all the things below?

■ Underline all the verbs to show what they have done to be so helpful. The first one has been done for you.

1. I <u>have finished</u> my homework.
2. I have washed the dishes.
3. I have cleaned the bathroom.
4. I have cooked dinner for everyone.
5. I have fed the cat and I have put the empty tin in the recycling bin.
6. I have watered the plants and I have mowed the lawn.

■ If we were talking about the girl we could say *She has finished her homework.* Write each of the sentences in this way – talking about what the girl has done. What would you write for a boy? What about for two or more people?

1. *She has finished her homework.*
2. ______________________________
3. ______________________________
4. ______________________________
5. ______________________________
6. ______________________________

Nag, nag, nag

■ Answer each of the questions below using a sentence. The first one has been done for you.

1. Have you eaten your breakfast?

Yes, I have eaten my breakfast.

2. Have you done your homework?

3. Have you tidied your room?

4. Have you cleaned your teeth?

5. Have you fed the pets?

6. Have you said goodnight to everyone?

■ Now write some questions using these verbs, and then try them on your friends.

closed finished told been seen

Tense spotting

Objective

To consider different verb tenses in writing.

Background knowledge

While in theory it is not too difficult to explain how verbs are formed for different tenses, their actual use and variation in texts suitable for young children can be complex and, as with much grammar, children can easily understand the meaning conveyed while finding it difficult to 'deconstruct' the grammar involved.

In looking at texts to identify verbs and tenses, as well as change these tenses, anomalies and unusual cases will crop up regularly. As such, the activities below are suggested to gently raise children's awareness of the role of verbs and verb tenses in shaping meanings, as well as bringing the language of the relevant grammar slightly more into focus.

Activities

- **Photocopiable page 71 'Alien lesson'**

This activity challenges the children to match examples to definitions of tenses as a way of familiarising them with grammatical explanations. It is a suitable individual or whole-class activity, when you might model appropriate language and elicit further examples from the class.

- **Photocopiable page 72 'Just like Johnny'**

This is a tricky activity intended to raise children's awareness of using adverbs with the present perfect. Children will do this easily in everyday speech and reading, but they may need additional support to understand the construction of negatives and other expressions that use adverbs that change the meaning of the verb.

- **Photocopiable page 73 'Spot the tense'**

Here, the children are asked to create a colour key for the four tenses considered so far (although please note the reference to 'future' in the background knowledge on page 62) and to shade examples of each tense in the story. This activity is complex for children in two ways: the tenses are, to a degree, intermingled and their use is subtle and dependent on the circumstance of the story; and there are infinitives present. This is best left unexplained for the moment; more important is that they recognise the forms that they have recently encountered.

Further ideas

- **Tense check:** Continually check the tenses in which different texts are written. As the children encounter a report text, a recount or persuasion, encourage them to reflect on why a particular tense suited the subject matter. Look out for interesting examples – a lot of jokes are written and said in the present tense: *A man walks into a bar… ouch!*
- **Tense switching:** Switch sentences between tenses. During shared or guided writing, as the children are devising various sentences, ask them to consider what it would be like if it were written in a different tense. There is no need to write these – but they are worth sharing quickly and verbally.

Digital content

On the digital component you will find:

- Printable versions of all three photocopiable pages.
- Answers to 'Alien lesson' and 'Spot the tense'.
- Interactive version of 'Alien lesson'.

Alien lesson

■ Someone has been trying to explain to aliens how different verb tenses work but they haven't been doing very well. Can you match the explanations to the right examples? Draw a line between them.

Explanations	Examples
The present tense is used to talk about things that are happening now, or for giving commands.	Last year we went to London.
The past tense is used to talk about things that have finished.	I will see you tomorrow.
The future is used to talk about things that have not yet happened.	I have finished my breakfast.
The present perfect is used for things that happened in the past but are still important.	Please stand up.
	We will go out after dinner.
	I live in England.
	We arrived yesterday evening.
	He has been ill all day.

Name:

Tense spotting

Just like Johnny

■ Look at these statements about Johnny. Each one uses the present perfect because it is about his life until now.

■ Look at the words in bold – these are adverbs, and go between 'has' and the main verb.

He has **just** finished his lunch.

He has **not** remembered his homework.

He has **never** eaten asparagus.

He has **always** walked to school.

He has **sometimes** wondered if there is life on Mars.

■ Can you write some sentences about yourself? Begin each one with *I have*, and then choose new verbs and adverbs or use the ones above.

I have ______________________________

I have ______________________________

I have ______________________________

I have ______________________________

I have ______________________________

I have ______________________________

Tense spotting

Spot the tense

■ Read this article from a local newspaper. Choose four coloured pencils and complete the key, then shade each example of present, past, present perfect and future for all the verbs you can find.

Key

Tense/time	Colour
Present	
Past	
Present perfect	
Future	

Tumbletown News

No supper shock for local schoolboy

Tommy Tucker, the naughtiest schoolboy in town, went to bed without food last night. He refused to sing for his supper and his mother sent him to bed immediately. She then ate all of their pie herself.

Our ace reporter, Mary Lamb, spoke to Tommy this morning. "It is not fair!" said Tommy. "For years now I have sung for my supper. I have entertained my family and friends with my songs since I was five! It was the first time ever that I have said no, and what has happened? I have not eaten anything since teatime yesterday!"

Sadly, it looks like Tommy's troubles are not yet over. He will miss his break today because he has not finished his homework. "It will be chips for lunch too," cried Tommy, "and I will be in the classroom doing sums. My teacher will force me to stay in, and will not let me eat my dinner. It is not fair!"

We tried to speak to Tommy's teacher, Mr Wolf, but he was not available. He was on a school trip to the woods, apparently.

Verbs in writing

Objective

To develop the use of verbs and verb tenses in writing.

Writing focus

Building on previous activities about verbs and verb tenses, this section encourages children to expand their use of verbs and helps them to secure their choice and use of tense across a range of pieces of writing.

Skills to writing

- **Try a verb on**

Trying a new word is never as simple as substituting one word found in a thesaurus for another. As children encounter new words for an action like 'speak', they need to know the difference between a synonym like 'tell' and one like 'accost'. As they encounter new verbs, encourage them to 'try them on', seeking out opportunities for the new word over the course of a school day or in the texts they encounter – possibly even tallying up the amount of use it receives.

- **Imperative instructing**

Use of the imperative verb is an important feature of instructional writing. Again, verbs can provide a good planning tool, with children itemising these as a way of staging out the process they will be writing. Watch out for children writing activities they know well or have done as instructional texts – it is very common for them to lapse into an 'I'-based past-tense narrative mode.

- **Imagining verbs**

Building up the stock of verbs that children can draw on for their writing is one of the key ways of enriching the language they use. However, you cannot simply impose a list of new verbs on children. This just ends up with the words being used inappropriately or sounding stilted and wooden. To expand children's verb bank it is important to allow them to become familiar with the new words, say them aloud and enjoy the sound. Verbs such as 'pounded' are a pleasure to say. You also need to make sure that the children know their meaning: 'pounded' isn't a straight synonym of 'knocked', it's a particular type of knock. A good way for children to learn the meaning of verbs is to picture or act them (have a go at pounding!). To help the children consolidate the information, try out the words in drama as well as shared, modelled and guided writing – new words need to be given an airing!

- **Tense and text type**

Encourage the children to look at the tenses in texts. As they encounter different texts, ask them to keep a tally of how the texts use different tenses. Ask why such language suits the purpose – for example, there's a good reason a newsletter often recounts in the past tense and a trip letter anticipates an outing in the future. One interesting feature to look out for is the way a single text can mix the tenses; for example, a letter that says what the children have been doing could then slip into a future class assembly.

Activities

- **Photocopiable page 76 'School trip'**

This activity raises awareness of the present perfect tense and the future, with two brief texts referring to the same trip to be sorted into logical order. A further challenge is then presented to produce a recount of the trip in the past tense – this is probably best done separately and with a modelled introduction. The activity could easily be extended by producing further statements from the 'future' letter to set scenarios, challenging the children to create further text messages showing the immediate outcomes.

- **Photocopiable page 77 'Adventurous verbs'**

A selection of regular verbs is presented along with reminders of tenses and a selection of genres that children may be familiar with. This resource can be used for individual, group or whole-class work depending on the focus of the teacher and the needs of the class.

Write on

- **School of the future**

Practise writing in the future by producing imaginative report texts on what it will be like in the school of the future. How will children travel there? What will lessons look like? What sort of teachers will they have? What will happen at playtime? As the children write up their future texts, they could also consider what might be the same. What won't change over the coming 100 years?

- **Imagine being them**

Choose a character from a familiar book and list the key events that happen to them. Challenge the children to write a short piece that uses the information but in a different form, such as a diary entry for the past, a text-message-type running commentary using the present perfect. Ask them to imagine what might happen next – from the characters' point of view – to use the future tense.

- **Top spies**

This activity can be done in real life, with the teacher acting out scenarios to the class, or linked to the previous idea of using familiar texts. Ask the children to imagine that they are in a secret location – up a tree, in a nearby building, in a hot-air balloon, or even using a magic mirror. They are observing the actions of a person or character and have to relay the recent actions back to headquarters through a walkie-talkie or via text-type messages: He has left the building, He has finished his lunch and so on. Note that there will be inevitable confusion and the automatic use of other tenses (for example, *She is running away*) and you will need to deal with this as appropriate.

- **Questions, questions**

Ask the children to write, in each of the tenses, a question that they will ask of a classmate to gather information about them. Remind them that the tense will help demonstrate the type of information they wish to gather about the person they are interviewing (for example, the present tense will establish a permanent feature/fact). Work initially with the class to develop suitable questions that can be asked to yourself and write these on the board, then model appropriate answers. The activity can then be conducted as an oral or written exercise.

Digital content

On the digital component you will find:

- Printable versions of both photocopiable pages.
- Answers to 'School trip'.

Name:

Verbs in writing

School trip

■ There are two short texts all jumbled up below. One is a letter about a school trip to the seaside, the other is a series of text messages sent by one of the teachers on the trip. Can you sort out the different texts and put them into the right order?

We have played football and rounders all afternoon! ☺
We will eat lunch as soon as we arrive.
We have eaten our sandwiches – they were full of sand! LOL!
Everyone has eaten an ice cream. I have had two! ☺
We will arrive at the seaside at noon.
We have arrived, thank goodness – everyone needs the loo. LOL!
We will play games until 3pm.
The bus will leave school at 9am sharp.
Hurray! We have left school. I have forgotten my suncream. ☹
If there is time we will have an ice cream before we come home.

■ For a further challenge, imagine it is the next day at school. Write a story in the past tense about the trip. Make it as fun as you like, but include all the information from the letter and text messages.

Verbs in writing

Adventurous verbs

■ Can you use these interesting verbs in your writing, perhaps for some kind of adventure?

■ Here are some genres you might use:

- **Past tense:** diary, newspaper report.
- **Present perfect:** live text messages or news report.
- **Future:** a report or letter explaining future plans.

yell	whisper	explore	launch
gasp	scramble	scream	crunch
frown	startle	uncover	jump

They are all regular verbs, so remember:

1. The past tense adds 'ed'. If the verb ends in 'e' just add 'd'.
For example: *Startled, she slowly uncovered the strange plant.*

2. The future uses 'will'.
For example: *We will explore the area tomorrow.*

3. The present perfect uses 'have' plus the verb with 'ed'.
For example: *The aliens have seized our leader; we have launched our escape rocket.*

Chapter 4

Sentences

Introduction

The grammatical rules of single and multi-clause sentences can be hard for young children to grasp, even though they will most probably have encountered a wide range of sentence constructions in their reading, and indeed will be using them in their everyday conversations.

This chapter gradually introduces the concept of clauses and the role that conjunctions, prepositions and adverbs have in joining them. Through this the children will learn how to improve their sentence writing using expressions of time, cause and place, which is the focus of the subsequent section. For further practice, please see the 'Sentences' section of the Year 3 workbook.

In this chapter

Clauses page 81	To identify clauses.
Linking clauses page 85	To use a range of conjunctions.
Conjunctions, adverbs and prepositions page 89	To understand the function of conjunctions, adverbs and prepositions.
Showing time, place and cause page 93	To express time, place and cause.
Improving sentence writing page 97	To improve sentence writing by incorporating conjunctions, adverbs and prepositions.

Poster notes

Clauses (page 79)
The poster contains a simple explanation of what clauses are and demonstrates how subordinate clauses help main clauses, introducing a small range of conjunctions.

Time, cause and, place (page 80)
This provides a bank of words that can act as conjunctions. Its aim is to increase familiarity with such words and to be available as a support for children's own thinking and writing as they complete activities and develop their own texts.

Vocabulary

Children should already know:
noun phrase, statement, question, exclamation, command

In Year 3 children need to know:
prefix, article (definite and indefinite), word family, consonant, consonant letter, vowel, vowel letter

Sentences

CLAUSES

Simple or single-clause sentences contain one clause. **Example:** *The school trip was cancelled.*
Some have another clause to explain things a bit more. **Example:** *The school trip was cancelled because **it was raining**.*
The bold example is a subordinate clause – it helps the main clause. Clauses are often joined with conjunctions such as 'because', 'as', 'but', 'or' and so on.

Here are some more examples. Can you pick out the main clause, the subordinate clause and the conjunction in each sentence?

Most people love baby animals because they are so cute.

The teacher searched for the ball but someone had hidden it.

Put on your coat and wellies or you will get wet.

The school football match was cancelled as the other team didn't turn up.

Sentences

Time, cause and place

There is a range of words that help us to be clear when we talk about things. These words help us to be clear about time (for example 'before'), cause (for example 'because') and place (for example 'inside').
Look at the words on this poster and decide what they can help to explain. Some are opposites – can you spot them?

Clauses

Objective

To identify clauses.

Background knowledge

The focus of this section is to introduce and familiarise children with the concept of clauses, moving on to subordinate clauses. At this stage teachers should not be over-concerned with children appreciating the difference between single and multi-clause sentences (some multi-clause sentences have two clauses and both make sense independent of the other; some have a main clause and subordinate clause, and the subordinate clause does not make sense without the main one).

Conjunctions are covered in greater depth later in the chapter, but they are worth touching on as they can help children to understand and spot the link between clauses.

Activities

- **Photocopiable page 82 'What is a clause?'**

This activity asks the children to find the clauses in sentences. The sentences provide some fairly clear-cut examples of clauses. To support their learning, the children are first asked to identify the conjunctions joining the clauses (there are one or two sentences with more than one conjunction). Note that subordinate clauses are not introduced at this stage.

- **Photocopiable page 83 'Sentence repairs'**

In this activity, children match the clauses to rebuild a broken sentence. Once they have done this they can reflect on which parts of the rebuilt sentence can stand independently. For example, in *Shona had a leaving party so that we could all say 'Goodbye' to her*, the first half of the sentence ('Shona had a leaving party') makes sense on its own whereas the second half does not. The first half is the main clause, and the second half is a subordinate clause that explains the reason behind the party.

- **Photocopiable page 84 'Subordinate clauses'**

This activity asks the children to look at the main and subordinate clauses in various sentences. It is worth spending some time with the class exploring how a main clause is one that can stand on its own, whereas a sub-clause is dependent upon the main clause to make sense. Although quite complex for this age-range, children usually master this once the penny drops, and it is an important step in developing their understanding of sentence structure.

Further ideas

- **Cutting out sentences:** Using disposable texts, such as leaflets and adverts, children can cut up the sentences they find into separate clauses.
- **Clause shading:** Children can look at texts and try finding some of the clauses contained in the sentences. They can then shade over these in different colours.
- **Crazy sentences:** Re-use photocopiable page 83 to see which clauses can be matched to make sentences that are crazy but grammatically correct (for example, *It was sunny so our teacher was not pleased. Because of the rain my Dad decided to have a haircut.*) Children can then try making their own sets of sentences with clauses to be separated and shuffled, considering each sentence carefully so that when the shuffling around takes place strange sentences start to appear.

Digital content

On the digital component you will find:

- Printable versions of all three photocopiable pages.
- Answers to all three photocopiable pages.
- Interactive version of 'Subordinate clauses'.

 Name:

Clauses

What is a clause?

Clauses are like a little sentence in themselves.
Some short sentences are made up of just one clause:

The dog barked.

Longer sentences can have more than one clause:

The dog barked	and	the cat ran away.

Clauses can be linked by conjunctions such as 'and'.

■ Look at these sentences. First, underline the conjunction in each one (the first three have been done for you), then cut out the separate clauses.

The cat sat still <u>and</u> the dog played the piano.
The dog was surprised <u>because</u> the cat started singing.
The dog covered his ears <u>so</u> he couldn't hear the cat.
The cat was pleased and she sang louder.
The dog caught a train but the cat followed him onto it.
The dog hid under a seat so the cat couldn't see him.
The dog got off the train before the cat could find him.
The cat gave up singing and she became a pianist.
The dog became a train driver and he gave up the piano.

Clauses

Sentence repairs

■ Match the beginnings and endings of the sentences below.

Beginning	Ending
The classroom was messy	my brother wore his wet trainers.
It was sunny	so our teacher was not pleased.
We made sandwiches	so that we could all say 'goodbye' to her.
By next Tuesday	my bike will be mended.
After thinking about it for ages,	my dad decided to have a haircut.
Because of the rain,	because we were having a picnic.
Even after he had been told not to,	although the forecast predicted rain.
Shona had a leaving party	our trip was cancelled.

Name:

Subordinate clauses

■ Read each of the sentences below and shade the subordinate clause in each one. The first one has been done for you.

The children made a cake because **they were having a party.**

If you want a good laugh, you should read my story.

After writing their stories, the children made a play.

The girl looked for her shoes as she had lost them.

If the weather improves we can play rounders.

When the clock says three o'clock, we can pack up for home.

Before going into assembly, we have to line up.

Our teacher, a very scruffy man, wore a tie today.

My mum, who's a vet, works in the city.

Josh found, after trying and trying, he could swim a whole length.

Linking clauses

Objective

To use a range of conjunctions.

Background knowledge

Clauses are usually linked by conjunctions. There are two types of conjunction: coordinating conjunctions link words or phrases together as equal pairs; subordinating conjunctions introduce a subordinate clause. Children do not need to understand the distinction at this stage. The main thing for them to recognise is that different conjunctions have different purposes. Conjunctions can:

- add one thing to another: *I like rain and I like snow.*
- oppose one thing to another: *I like rain but my friend hates it.*
- show how one thing is caused by another: *I like snow because it looks great.*
- show how one thing is linked to the time of another: *We'll build a snowman when we go outside.*

Activities

- **Photocopiable page 86 'Join the sentences'**
As they join up the separated sentences on this photocopiable sheet children will be guided by the conjunction that starts the second half of the sentence.
- **Photocopiable page 87 'Missing words'**
In choosing the right conjunction children will need to consider the job that should be done in the space within each sentence. This will guide them to choose between, for example, a 'but' and a 'because'.
- **Photocopiable page 88 'Making the connection'**
The completion of the sentences in this activity is directed by the conjunction at the end of the opening section. Once they have completed the photocopiable sheet, children could try re-doing one of their completed examples with the conjunction altered (for example *I could eat you but…*, *I could eat you and…*).

Further ideas

- **Find examples:** Children can find a variety of words that connect one thing to another or show the relationship between one thing and another.
- **And:** Focus on the use of the word 'and' – ask the children to look through their own uses of 'and' in their story writing. Could they have used a better alternative?
- **Favourite conjunctions:** The class can choose a conjunction to promote. They can try to slip it into their speech and writing. For example, they could adopt the word 'because' then use it as often as possible.
- **Altered meanings:** As suggested for follow-up work to photocopiable page 88 'Making the connection', children can take sentences that contain a conjunction, and either choose an alternative or pick one at random, then rewrite one of the clauses to ensure it makes sense.

Digital content

On the digital component you will find:

- Printable versions of all three photocopiable pages.
- Answers to 'Join the sentences' and 'Missing words'.
- Interactive version of 'Join the sentences'.

Name:

Linking clauses

Join the sentences

■ Cut out and repair these broken sentences. Find a second clause to match every first clause.

■ Underline or shade the conjunctions that join the clauses.

First clause	Second clause
I opened my umbrella	if you want them to grow.
We went to the library	because it was raining.
You need to water seeds	so I played on the slide.
Someone was on the swings	because the chain is broken.
We waited in the car	or a school dinner?
Joe looked for us	so I can buy a computer game.
I had my breakfast	until it is my birthday.
I can't wait	before I went to school.
Would you like sandwiches	and Lara went in goal.
I put on my socks	but it was closed.
We played football	after counting to fifty.
I can't ride my bike	before my shoes.
I have to save my pocket money	if you want to go out to play.
We got dressed	after doing PE.
Tidy the classroom	while Mum went in the shop.

Missing words

■ Look at the spaces in these sentences. They are all words people said. They are real quotes.

■ Which conjunctions from the word box could fit? Write as many conjunctions as you think could fit in each space. Say them aloud to check if they sound right.

■ Try writing your own sentences using some of these conjunctions.

I had to go home [ ] it was bedtime.

We didn't play outside [ ] it was raining.

We had our sandwiches [ ] we got on the bus.

I like juice [ ] my mum likes tea.

We put water in the freezer [ ] it turned into ice.

You can have a biscuit [ ] some cake.

I have got a bike [ ] it isn't working.

I haven't seen my friend [ ] he moved house.

because
while
when
as
if
before
so
after
but
until
or

Name:

Linking clauses

Making the connection

■ Can you finish these sentences? Fill in words you think the characters might say.

■ List the conjunctions that connect the first part of each sentence to your added words.

Conjunctions, adverbs and prepositions

Objective

To understand the function of conjunctions, adverbs and prepositions.

Background knowledge

The grammar of conjunctions, adverbs and prepositions can be very complex, and teachers will need to take care not to muddle children. At this stage the most important factor is raising awareness of the role of these words. Many books and resources can provide further information about these terms and their uses, but there are often many exceptions, variations and additional complexities. In addition, some words change class according to their usage – they might be an adverb in some situations but not in others. As stated, for the moment a focus on the words themselves is sufficient.

Activities

- **Photocopiable page 90 'Possible prepositions'**

This is a straightforward activity to allow children to incorporate a range of prepositions in sentences. The task can be extended by asking them to list two possible prepositions per sentence (the spaces on the sheet allow for this), as well as discussing possibilities with each other. Interesting reflection can also be generated by orally stating each sentence using the wrong preposition. Although children may not be ready to discuss the actual terms, incongruities often occur through using spatial or temporal prepositions inappropriately.

- **Photocopiable page 91 'Using adverbs'**

This is a trickier activity, which introduces children to adverbs of time and place. You may prefer to do this with the whole class, displaying the text and indicating words on the whiteboard. The main point to discuss and consider is how these words relate to verbs, and how they enhance the meaning by helping us to visualise events more clearly.

- **Photocopiable page 92 'Conjunction dice'**

Ask the children to cut out the cube nets and turn them into dice (dice 2 contains trickier words). They should then create sentences using one or more conjunctions, perhaps collaborating with a partner to generate a small and interesting piece of writing. More confident learners might use these alongside an existing piece of writing. Taking their text, they should roll the dice and see whether they can use one of the two conjunctions that appear.

Further ideas

- **Word of the day:** From a bank of words start each day or English lesson with a suitable conjunction displayed on the board, and ask children to generate three sentences.
- **Preposition questions:** Ask the children to quiz another child or an adult about the events of the previous day and try to come up with as many questions containing temporal prepositions, for example: *What did you do after breakfast? What were you reading before you sat in the classroom?* Initially teachers may prefer to work with the whole class to model examples and note prepositions and verb tenses.
- **Counting types:** Provide the children with different types of text and ask them to look through them carefully to see if certain conjunctions feature more in some texts than in others – for example, they may find explanatory texts have more causal connections and narratives more temporal ones.

Digital content

On the digital component you will find:

- Printable versions of all three photocopiable pages.
- Answers to 'Using adverbs'.
- Interactive version of 'Using adverbs'.

Name:

Conjunctions, adverbs and prepositions

Possible prepositions

■ Fill in two possible prepositions that could complete each sentence.

Wash the paint pots ______ playtime.

The football was ______ the shelf.

I found my pencil ______ the book.

The brush was 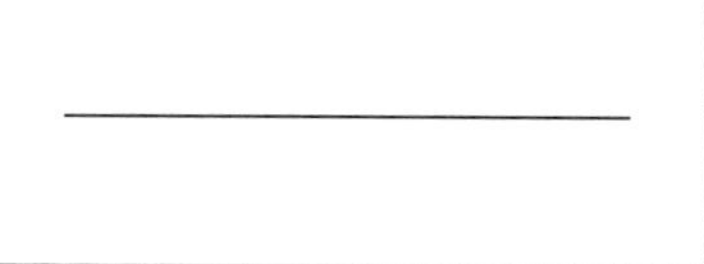 the paint pot.

Put the bottle 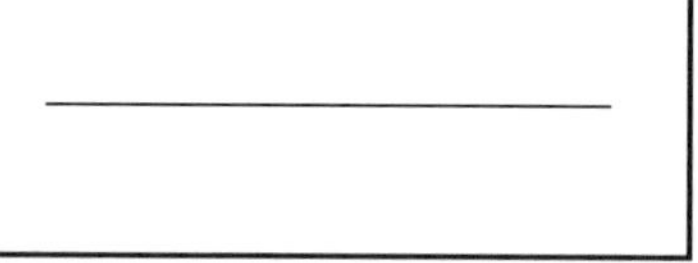 the sink.

I met Joe  the library.

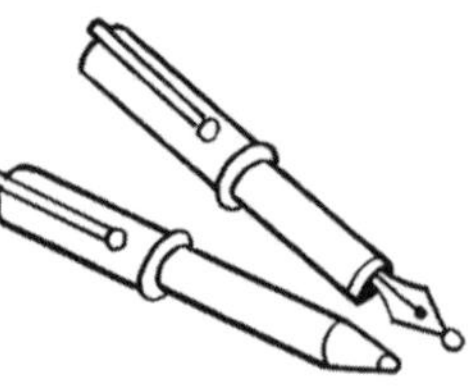

We had something to eat  playing outside.

Using adverbs

Some adverbs help us to explain time a bit more: *I will leave tomorrow*, and some are about position: *I sat beside him*.

■ Look at the short passage below and underline any words that tell you about time or position. The first two have been done for you.

She arrived <u>before</u> the others. She was riding <u>on</u> a large white horse. She had been waiting since twelve o'clock, standing outside the house. She saw a wolf coming near to the house. It was running through the trees, showing its sharpened fangs. In the past she would have panicked, but she was calm now. She looked into the eyes of the wolf. She stared until it stopped moving and was still. After a few minutes it turned around and walked away, trotting back into the woods. It went behind a tree and was gone. She waited until everything was silent again, climbed onto her horse, and rode towards the sunset.

Name:

Conjunction dice

■ Make two dice using these nets. Roll the dice while you are writing and see what conjunctions you get. Dice 2 is trickier than dice 1. Can you use them in a sentence?

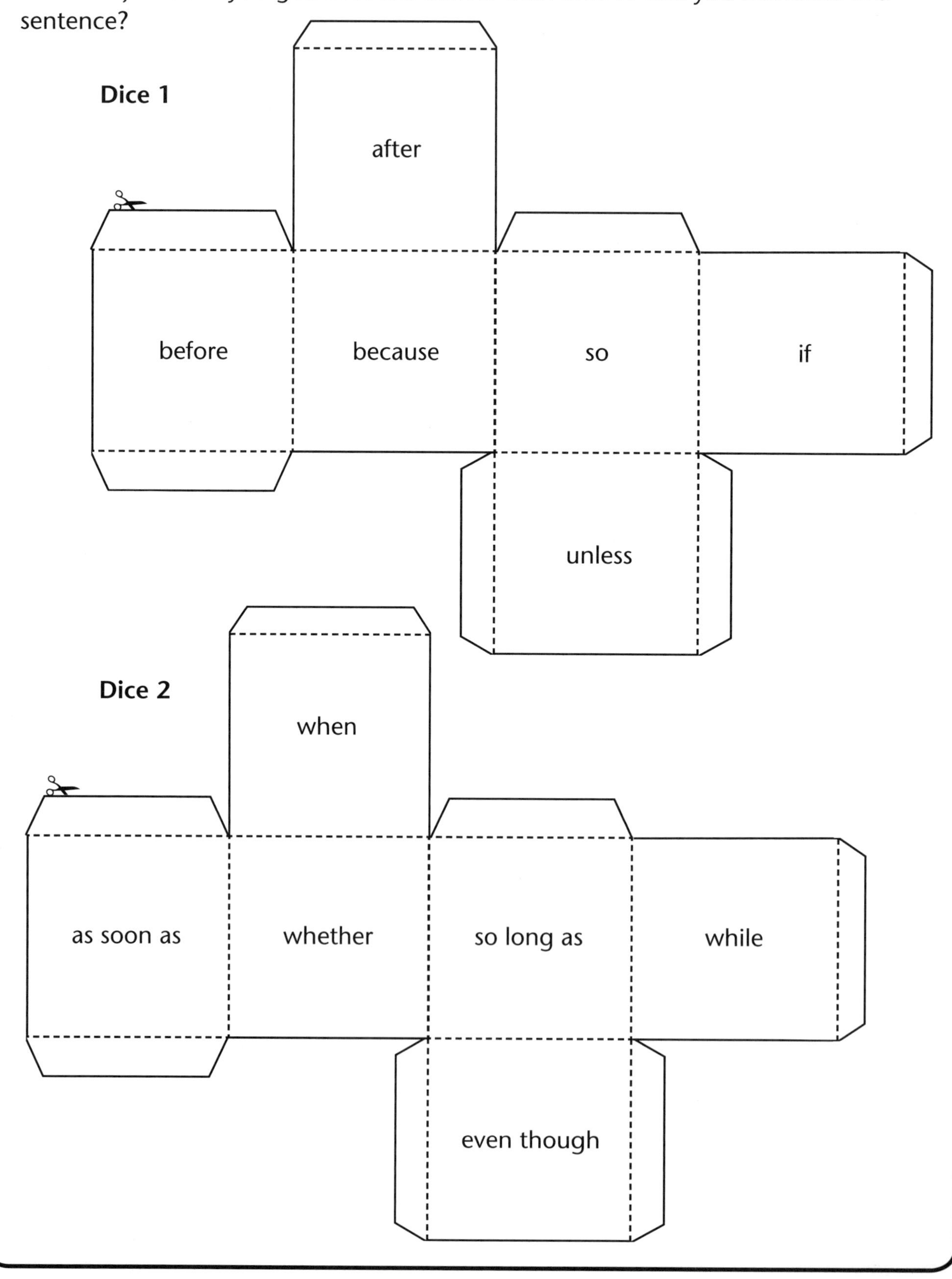

Showing time, place and cause

Objective

To express time, place and cause.

Background knowledge

This section moves to a greater focus of considering how conjunctions, adverbs and prepositions are used to express and convey meaning about time, place and cause. The poster on page 80 contains a selection of such words, though these are not grouped according to class or function. At this stage it is enough for children to develop awareness of their roles in shaping texts.

Activities

- **Photocopiable page 94 'Same start, different ending...'**

The different conjunctions should prompt children to produce different sentence endings. The various sentences can be discussed to examine how the conjunctions, adverbs and prepositions steer the various sentences in particular ways. In particular, in reviewing work with the class, highlight the linking word or phrase and consider whether time, place or cause was the focus of each sentence, then relate it to the word used.

- **Photocopiable page 95 'Where's Polly?'**

This activity offers reinforcement in the use of conjunctions, adverbs and prepositions to indicate the 'spatial' relation of objects. The exercise is relatively open in that children can choose both the location and the verb involved. In discussing work afterwards reinforce how different words indicate the spatial relationship of Polly to the different objects, and consider alternative ways of expressing this.

- **Photocopiable page 96 'Dear diary'**

This activity offers reinforcement in the use of conjunctions, adverbs and prepositions to explain the 'temporal' relationship of events, creating a diary that uses a selection of words appropriately to show the order of events. To begin the activity use the picture clues around the sheet to prompt ideas for events and their sequence, as well as discussing children's own unique daily activities to ensure a variety of diaries.

Further ideas

- **Time word telling:** Time words (such as the ones used on photocopiable page 96 'Dear diary') can be written on cards and placed on a table, face downwards. Groups then have the task of telling a story, sentence by sentence. One child starts with an opening. The next one follows, but first he or she must select one of the cards and then use the selected word as the starter for the sentence. This can send the story forwards, backwards, all over the place!
- **I, robot:** A fun game for practising use and understanding of spatial words is to set up a small range of equipment and objects, ideally in the hall or playground, and have children take turns in directing one another as to where to go and what to do.
- **It's not my fault:** In discussion, generate a list of things that can happen around the house: making a mess, breaking a plate, and so on. Model examples of excuses (as far-fetched as you like) using causal words such as *when*, *so*, *because*, and then challenge children to create their own.

Digital content

On the digital component you will find:

- Printable versions of all three photocopiable pages.

Name:

Showing time, place and cause

Same start, different ending...

- Using the sentence starters below, complete the sentences. The first one is done for you.
- How does the conjunction affect the way you finish the sentence?

The girl opened the box after	the postman had given it to her.
The girl opened the box so that	
The girl opened the box during	
The girl opened the box when	

We enjoy playtime but	
We enjoy playtime before	
We enjoy playtime because	
We enjoy playtime then	

The magician appeared when	
The magician appeared in order that	
The magician appeared beside	
The magician appeared from	

Showing time, place and cause

Where's Polly?

■ For each image draw Polly and write a sentence that uses a conjunction, adverb or preposition to show where she is. An example has been done for you. Try to write five very different sentences.

Name:

Showing time, place and cause

Dear diary

■ Some words tell us about how things happen compared to other things. For example, in the sentence: *I had a cup of tea then I went to the shops*, the word 'then' tells us that the visit to the shops came after the cup of tea; and in the sentence *I did my homework while my bath was running*, the word 'while' tells us that the homework and the bath were happening at the same time.

■ Write a diary of your day using some of these words to help you. Remember to use them to show how one thing came before another. Try to use each word once.

before	after	while	then	until	during	since	as soon as	when

Improving sentence writing

Objective

To improve sentence writing by incorporating conjunctions, adverbs and prepositions.

Writing focus

Drawing on the words and concepts developed in this chapter, the following activities encourage children to reflect on the way sentences are structured with a view towards revising their own writing.

Skills to writing

- **Sequencing**

Sequencing activities are important for children's grasp of story structure, instructions and explanations. When doing these activities, highlight the role played by conjunctions in structuring such texts.

- **Instructions**

When writing instructional texts, children should be encouraged to draw on a range of temporal conjunctions. Causal conjunctions can be highlighted as children encounter explanation texts, in which one phenomenon is caused by or causes another.

- **Narratives and conjunctions**

Use temporal conjunctions as a means of stimulating narrative writing. When planning a narrative task, draw the children's attention to two conjunctions that may feature in their thinking and planning. For example, if the word 'because' is highlighted, the children will think about the cause and effect of their plot, whereas a word such as 'after' will stimulate them to think of the events that follow, one after the other.

- **Clauses! Clauses! Clauses!**

Clauses are vital. Children need to understand what a clause is, to identify clauses in reading and be mindful of them in writing. Clauses are the main way in which children can extend their own sentence writing. Understanding the nature of clauses allows children to connect them effectively or separate them with commas as desired.

- **Persuasive connections**

Look out for the connections that are made in persuasive texts. Words such as 'therefore' and 'so' help a writer to make a case. Children should be encouraged to use appropriate conjunctions in their own writing of persuasive texts. They should aim to structure their case so that a 'because' argues back to evidence or a 'therefore' hammers home the thrust of their case.

- **Conjunctions in non-fiction**

Take note of the sort of conjunctions used in non-fiction texts. This can include looking at the use of causal conjunctions in explanatory texts, oppositional conjunctions in argument texts and temporal conjunctions in narrative. You can expand this activity by looking at the stylistic features of certain well-known texts, such as investigating what types of conjunction dominate football reports or instructions for playing a game. The experience of listening and picking apart sentences can attune children to their structure.

Activities

- **Photocopiable page 99 'Story stimulator'**

The connecting words chosen on the planner provide children with some stimulation for their story writing. This should be used alongside regular planning and isn't a substitute for it. By structuring story sentences around the word 'because', for example, the children will be able to reflect on a causal connection in their planned narrative. Once they have completed the planner, children should read it through to consider whether any of the structures they have recorded stimulate addition to, or alteration of, their story.

- **Photocopiable page 100 'Goldilocks confesses'**

This task extends some of the activities from earlier in the chapter, asking the children to develop interesting reasons and excuses for Goldilocks' misbehaviour. Ensure that the children have access to appropriate wordbanks as desired (see the poster on page 80), and encourage them to use a different word in each sentence (perhaps using the conjunction dice on page 92). This activity can be extended by asking the children to use the sentences they generate as a plan for a more flowing piece of prose, such as a letter of apology, a newspaper article and so on.

Write on

- **Ice the cake**

In editing and reviewing work, one way of developing the use of conjunctions, adverbs and prepositions is to ask the children if they can revise their writing like putting the icing on the cake to make it even more appealing. If they have written *I went to the park*, can they think why they went, or add something interesting about the journey? For example: *I was bored so I went to the park* or *I went to the park even though it was raining*.

- **Sentence expansion**

Ask the children to write single-clause sentences on strips of paper and then look to see where an extra clause could be inserted. As they do this they can cut up the sentence, add a strip in one place, and insert one in another. Make sure that they stick down and display their modified versions as this provides an effective reminder of how writers can rejig sentences.

- **Clause partners**

No, it's not Santa's new firm of solicitors but children working in pairs to develop clauses! Two children writing sentences together can be an effective way of pushing for more extended sentences. As they engage in their writing, each child in a pair needs to become a clause in a sentence. If the text is a persuasive piece and one of them is suggesting they should write *Fruit is good for you*, the second person needs to suggest how they could insert a clause in the sentence (for example, *because it is full of the things you need*). Somehow, two people sharing this task can make it plainer, as each of them physically becomes part of the sentence. Having a bank of appropriate words to hand will also be useful for stimulation and avoiding repetition.

- **Trios**

This activity is a way of developing children's use of words to connect clauses in writing. Each child takes a role. Child A acts as the conjunction, adverb or preposition, while the other two act as the parts of the sentence. Child B would be the part of the sentence before the word, and child C would be the part after it. So if the trio are working on a report about the school, child A may select 'so' as the connecting word. Child B will then think of something that could be written before 'so', such as 'the bell rings'. Child C then has to think of something to come after the 'so', making a sentence such as *The bell rings so we line up*. Children can take turns to play different parts as the text is developed.

Digital content

On the digital component you will find:

- Printable versions of both photocopiable pages.

Improving sentence writing

Story stimulator

■ Use this planner to devise ideas for a story. How could your story ideas be framed around these conjunctions? For example:

The candle went out ***when*** *the window blew open.*

when

and then

so

because

If then

Name:

Improving sentence writing

Goldilocks confesses

■ Look at each of the sentences below. Can you provide Goldilocks with good reasons for her actions? Try not to repeat any of the words that connect the phrases. The first one has been done for you.

 1. I went into the woods for a walk after my breakfast.	 2. I went into the cottage ______________
 3. I tried the big bowl of porridge ______________	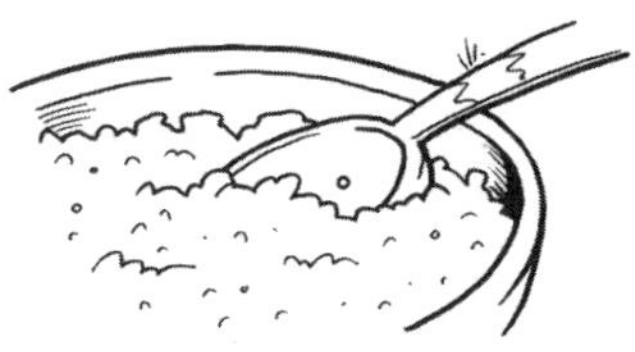 4. I tried the medium bowl of porridge ______________
 5. I ate the small bowl of porridge ______________	 6. I went upstairs ______________
 7. I tried the big bed ______________	 8. I tried the medium-sized bed ______________
 9. I fell asleep in the little bed ______________	 10. I jumped out of the bedroom window and ran home ______________

Chapter 5

Organising texts

Introduction

This chapter develops and extends children's understanding of structuring texts for different purposes. Using fiction and non-fiction texts, the chapter considers the use of paragraphs and other organisational devices to structure longer texts logically and effectively, making them easier to read and follow. In particular, the flow between paragraphs and the accurate choice of headings and subheadings is developed through focused activities and a range of ideas for classroom tasks. For further practice, please see the 'Organising texts' section of the Year 3 workbook.

Poster notes

Paragraphs (page 102)
This poster provides a simple explanation of paragraphs, followed by a letter to highlight this. Note that it does not cover direct speech.
Headings and subheadings (page 103)
This poster exemplifies how to use headings, subheadings and simple lists by providing information about how to use them. It can be displayed for children to refer to when tackling the activities and exercises in this chapter.

In this chapter

What is a paragraph? page 104	To understand how paragraphs are used to group related material.
Using paragraphs page 108	To begin to use paragraphs in writing.
Headings and subheadings page 112	To understand how headings and subheadings can be used to organise information.
Organising non-narrative writing page 116	To begin to use simple organisational devices in writing.
Planning and organising writing page 120	To use paragraphs and other organisational devices in writing.

Vocabulary

Children should already know:
capital letter, full stop, punctuation, sentence
In Year 3 children need to know:
paragraph, heading, subheading

Organising texts

PARAGRAPHS

A new paragraph always starts on a new line.

A paragraph is one or more sentences that share the same idea.

Paragraphs help us to organise information and ideas.

Dear Mum and Dad,

We arrived yesterday afternoon. The bus journey took ages. We all sang songs for a while but the teacher told us to be quiet. We ate lots of sweets and Timothy Perks was sick twice. The driver made us clean it up!

The campsite is not very nice. It is on a steep hill and the toilets are awful. The tents are old and full of holes.

I am sharing a tent with Timothy Perks and Jason Smith. I got almost no sleep because they both snored very loudly all night. Then this morning we were woken up at six o'clock by a cockerel.

I have to finish writing because we are going on a ten-mile walk in the pouring rain. I hope my flip-flops will be ok for walking in.

Lots of love,
Billy xxx

Look at this letter from a homesick boy. Can you see what each paragraph is about?

Organising texts

Headings and subheadings

There are different things we can do to make information texts easier to read. This poster explains some of them. You should be able to see a heading, a subheading and a list.

Headings

Headings explain to us the main subject of a text. They are usually the largest letters and are often bold.

Subheadings

These separate different parts of the text, and are like a title for each part. They are often bold and can be larger or the same size as the text below them.

There can be more than one paragraph under a subheading, and there is often a space before the next one.

Lists

Sometimes it is easier to provide information in lists. These can have numbers at the start, bullet points, lines or even arrows. Each item in a list can be a sentence or a word.

Lists are:

- useful for instructions
- great for showing ingredients for cooking
- ideal for listing equipment needed for tasks
- a quick way of presenting information.

What is a paragraph?

Objective

To understand how paragraphs are used to group related material.

Background knowledge

We encounter paragraphs in most texts. They are used in both fiction and non-fiction texts as a way of organising information to make its flow logical and meaningful. Paragraphs always start on a new line, including for a new speaker in dialogue, although dialogue is not the focus of this chapter.

Activities

- **Photocopiable page 105 'Boggis, Bunce and Bean'**

This photocopiable sheet provides the opening paragraphs from *Fantastic Mr Fox* to help illustrate the change of subject between paragraphs. Read this with the class and discuss the content of each paragraph and then summarise it, then discuss the length and detail of each paragraph in turn. Also point out the spacing between paragraphs and the use of punctuation to form complete sentences in each paragraph.

- **Photocopiable page 106 'Roald Dahl'**

This activity requires the children to read a brief biography of Roald Dahl and to summarise the focus of each paragraph. The focus of discussion will probably be around how to separate out overall focus from incidental detail, for example 'his school days' as opposed to 'he was unhappy at school'. Once again, use the text to consolidate the children's understanding of how paragraphs are presented: complete sentences, new line and so on.

- **Photocopiable page 107 'Ordering paragraphs'**

Children are provided with a jumbled synopsis of *The King of the Cloud Forest* by Michael Morpurgo. They must cut out and re-order the paragraphs to create a logical and meaningful text. This activity also introduces paragraph linking, and this can be noted when reviewing work along with discussing the main focus of each paragraph.

Further ideas

- **Cutting out paragraphs:** Using disposable texts, such as leaflets and simple newspaper articles, let the children cut up the paragraphs and challenge other children to rearrange them.
- **Summaries:** Using simple texts or excerpts from books, challenge the children to write a summary that consists of one sentence per paragraph.
- **Direct speech:** Although direct speech is not the focus of this chapter, children will inevitably notice that new speakers start a new paragraph when they are reading fiction. Treat this just as any other paragraph work – both of the ideas above can be used with text containing dialogue.
- **Linking paragraphs:** Not all texts contain links between paragraphs, though it is worth looking at such texts with the class to consider how this helps the flow of both reading and comprehension. In appropriate places use coloured pens or pencils to highlight the relevant words at the end and beginning of connecting paragraphs to show how the author achieves such linking.

Digital content

On the digital component you will find:

- Printable versions of all three photocopiable pages.
- Answers to 'Roald Dahl' and 'Ordering paragraphs'.

What is a paragraph?

Boggis, Bunce and Bean

■ Here are the opening paragraphs from *Fantastic Mr Fox* by Roald Dahl. Read them and think about how the author has organised the writing.

Down in the valley there were three farms. The owners of these farms had done well. They were rich men. They were also nasty men. All three of them were about as nasty and mean as any men you could meet. Their names were Farmer Boggis, Farmer Bunce and Farmer Bean.

Boggis was a chicken farmer. He kept thousands of chickens. He was enormously fat. This was because he ate three boiled chickens smothered with dumplings every day for breakfast, lunch and supper.

Bunce was a duck-and-goose farmer. He kept thousands of ducks and geese. He was a kind of pot-bellied dwarf. He was so short his chin would have been underwater in the shallow end of any swimming-pool in the world. His food was doughnuts and goose-livers. He mashed the livers into a disgusting paste and then stuffed the paste into the doughnuts. This diet gave him a tummy-ache and a beastly temper.

Bean was a turkey-and-apple farmer. He kept thousands of turkeys in an orchard full of apple trees. He never ate any food at all. Instead, he drank gallons of strong cider which he made from the apples in the orchard. He was as thin as a pencil and the cleverest of them all.

From *Fantastic Mr Fox* by Roald Dahl

Name:

What is a paragraph?

Roald Dahl

■ Read this short biography of Roald Dahl. Can you decide what the main subject of each paragraph is? Write it in each box.

Roald Dahl was born in Wales in 1916. His parents were both from Norway. He was one of six children. Although Norway was far away they used to go there for the summer holidays each year.

When he was only eight he was given the cane at school for putting a mouse into a jar of gob-stoppers, and after that he was sent to boarding school. He was unhappy at school because the discipline was very cruel. The only good bit was the sport – he was good at that. Also, there was a large chocolate factory nearby and sometimes they would send new chocolates for the schoolboys to try.

After leaving school Roald worked in Africa. It gave him the chance to see lots of wildlife like crocodiles and snakes. When he was 22 there was a terrible war and he had to help his country. He had an aeroplane crash in the desert in North Africa and cracked his skull. He started having very bad headaches and was sent to work in America, where he started writing stories.

As everyone knows, Roald went on to become one of the world's best-loved children's authors, writing famous books with unforgettable characters. Most were written by hand using a pencil and paper in a gypsy wagon in the garden of his house. Millions of copies of the books have been sold all around the world.

Roald was married twice and had five children. He died in 1990 but all the books he wrote will live on, making children from all around the world smile and laugh for many years to come.

What is a paragraph?

Ordering paragraphs

■ The paragraphs below are a summary of the first half of *The King of the Cloud Forest* by Michael Morpurgo. They are not in the correct order. Cut them out and sequence them correctly.

High in the Himalayas, blizzards strike. Ashley and Sung must shelter in a hut without food, and where wolves are scratching at the door. Desperately hungry, Uncle Sung tells Ashley to stay in the hut while he goes in search of food.
Ashley Anderson lives in China with his father, a Christian missionary. When the advancing Japanese soldiers threaten their peace, Ashley is forced to flee with his beloved Uncle Sung, a Tibetan Buddhist.
Ashley is cared for by the Yetis, but soon realises that they think he is someone very special, a King. What do the yetis want from him?
The journey they plan is immense and full of danger. It will take them over the Himalayan Mountains to Tibet, Nepal and then India. It seems impossible, and seems even more dangerous when Sung tells Ashley about the strange creatures called Yetis who are rumoured to live in the mountains.
Ashley senses he is not alone: strange shapes in the snow and hairy faces at the window terrify him. Dying of hunger he finds himself rescued by the Yetis and taken to live with them in a remote Cloud Forest.

Using paragraphs

Objective

To begin to use paragraphs in writing.

Background knowledge

Helping children to start incorporating paragraphs into their own writing can be tricky. They need to have sustained exposure to and practice with a variety of texts. They need to hear texts being read with pauses for sentences, and changes of inflection and tone for new paragraphs – and they need to practise reading texts in this way. In addition, they need to look at fiction and non-fiction texts and consider differences in the way paragraphs are used (for example, non-fiction texts tend to use adverbs or conjunctions to start paragraphs, such as 'first', 'next', 'finally', and so on).

Activities

- **Photocopiable page 109 'Paragraphs for non-fiction'**

This activity presents a sequence of pictures showing the stages of making toast. A word-bank at the bottom of the page provides subject-specific vocabulary as well as words to support children in starting new paragraphs. To introduce this, look at other non-fiction texts, particularly instructions, and how they sequence information.

- **Photocopiable page 110 'Paragraphs for fiction'**

Using a similar format to the previous activity, this photocopiable sheet provides children with a sequence of pictures telling the story of 'Little Red Riding Hood'. Story-specific vocabulary is included, but not conjunctions or prepositions as these tend to be used more for paragraphs in non-fiction. You may need to recap the main points of the story, even working with the class to consider the focus of each picture and to write captions to help support planning. Also, consider encouraging more confident learners to start thinking about linking their paragraphs.

- **Photocopiable page 111 'A letter to Marty's parents'**

This activity contains a list of naughty things that Marty has done in the classroom during the day, and when he did them. His exasperated teacher has handed it to the head teacher for a letter to be sent home. Children must take on the role of head teacher and send an appropriately worded letter to Marty's mum and dad, using paragraphs to outline each event. You may also wish to introduce and develop knowledge of letter-writing conventions.

Further ideas

- **Listen up:** When reading to the class, use pauses, tone and inflection to mark the change between paragraphs, and ask the class to try and notice when a new paragraph starts. After each page, display the book and discuss the paragraphs and transitions.
- **Read aloud:** The 'Listen up' activity can be progressed to children reading prepared short pieces using punctuation and paragraphs to affect their delivery.
- **Plan, plan, plan:** Even the most spontaneous of writers plan their work, even if it is just in their head. In working on children's planning skills for fiction and non-fiction, develop their competence in creating plans that act as a list of paragraph themes. The activity on photocopiable page 122 will help with this.

Digital content

On the digital component you will find:

- Printable versions of all three photocopiable pages.

Using paragraphs

Paragraphs for non-fiction

■ Look at these pictures showing how to make toast. Can you write a paragraph for each one? Try to give each paragraph at least two sentences.
There are some words at the bottom that might help you.

Useful words for toast	Useful words for paragraphs
bread, butter, knife, plate, toaster, toast	first, to begin, next, after, finally, to finish

Name:

Using paragraphs

Paragraphs for fiction

■ The sequence of pictures below tells the story of 'Little Red Riding Hood'. Can you write a paragraph for each picture to tell the story in your own words?

Useful words for your story
Little Red Riding Hood, woods, Grandma, cottage, wolf, woodcutter

Using paragraphs

A letter to Marty's parents

■ Marty Mason has been a bit of a nuisance today and his teacher has made some notes about what he has been up to. You must use these notes to write a letter home to Marty's mum and dad so that they can come to school to see you. Remember to use paragraphs to describe the different incidents.

Notes on Marty Mason.

9.30am - Marty stood up and started singing 'God Save the Queen' during assembly.
Morning break - Marty sneaked through the school railings and went to buy some crisps.
11am - We lost Marty again in maths. I found him in the art cupboard painting everything red.
Lunchtime - The dinner supervisor reported that Marty ate all of his lunch, all of someone else's, and then stuffed his pockets full of chips before running into the playground singing 'God save the Queen'.
2.30pm - During circle time Marty started throwing cold chips at everyone and singing 'God save the Queen' - it was pandemonium!

Begin your letter:
Dear Mr and Mrs Mason,
I hope that you will be able to come in to see me to discuss Marty's behaviour, which I'm afraid hasn't been very good today.

End your letter:
Many thanks for reading this. I hope you will be able to come to school soon so that we can help Marty to improve his behaviour.

Headings and subheadings

Objective

To understand how headings and subheadings can be used to organise information.

Background knowledge

Children will probably have come across many headings and subheadings in their encounters with non-fiction texts. Although these are quite straightforward to understand, they often have an effect on the style of writing and the impact of texts. Certainly, the importance of effective headlines is quite obvious, and the use of subheadings can make text easier to scan and appreciate. Interaction with age-appropriate newspapers, websites and information texts (leaflets, brochures, encyclopedias and so on) can all help.

Activities

- **Photocopiable page 113 'Headings and headlines'**
This photocopiable sheet provides a selection of headings and headlines to help exemplify the style and tone of language used. It can be displayed and each item discussed in turn. Ask: *What sort of text is it from? Where might we see it? What might the accompanying text be?* This can then be extended by looking at actual headings and headlines as appropriate.
- **Photocopiable page 114 'A guide to France'**
In this activity children have to indicate which subheadings belong where in a simple information leaflet. The main task is straightforward, and can be extended by considering alternative subheadings and/or discussing the text itself and how the information is conveyed. Before starting be sure to discuss and exemplify the purpose of subheadings.
- **Photocopiable page 115 'Looking at lists'**
This page provides a small selection of lists of different styles and focus. These can be used for discussion or writing tasks using appropriate prompts, such as: *What is the purpose of each list? Is it effective? Who might have created it? Can anything else be added? Can you create a similar list for a different purpose? What makes it different from the other lists?* and so on.

Further ideas

- **Lesson headlines:** At the end of the lesson, ask for contributions for the headline that best sums up the lesson, taking a class vote on the most apt.
- **Create subheadings:** Either using an appropriate text without headings or removing the subheadings from an existing text, challenge the class to insert their own headings and subheadings in the appropriate places. Discussing these afterwards can sharpen children's perception of how to choose meaningful and concise words.
- **Analysing texts:** Without looking at content, choose a wide range of texts from novels to newspapers and work with the class to quickly list the organisational features they contain: chapters, paragraphs, sentences, headings, subheadings, lists, and so on, perhaps creating a checklist for each text.

Digital content

On the digital component you will find:

- Printable versions of all three photocopiable pages.
- Answers to 'A guide to France'.

Headings and headlines

- Look at the selection of headings and headlines on this page and consider what each one is about. Where might you see words like this? What words might come after it?

United beat City 3–0!

The six wives of Henry VIII

Welcome to our hotel

Unit 6 – verbs

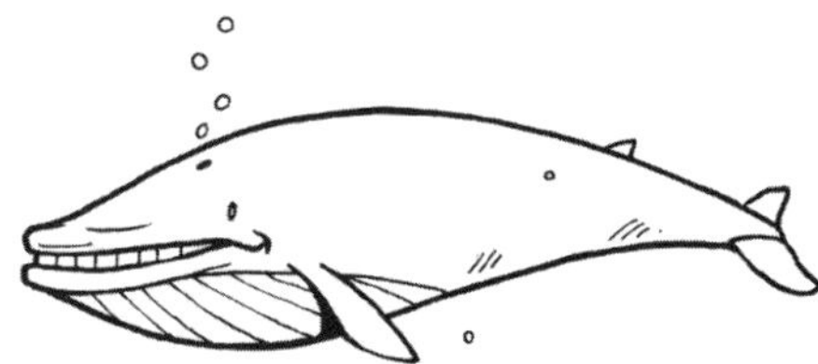

Whales

Missing cat found safe and well

Bake better cakes

Looking after your new bike

Name:

Headings and subheadings

A guide to France

■ This is a brief guide to France for British people who have never been there before. At the bottom of the page, there is one heading and four subheadings. Write them in the correct places.

___

You may never have been to France before, but you will probably know a bit about it. A country that is famous for its wine and food, France also has wonderful countryside, beautiful beaches, mountains and rivers. Some people say there are many different Frances, because it changes so much from place to place.

___

First, you have to get there. You can drive to France, taking your car on the ferries or through the tunnel; you can fly to France – there are lots of airports; or you can take the train. French trains are fast and punctual, and the roads are often quiet, but remember that the French drive on the other side of the road from us.

___

The French love food and are very proud of all the different foods they have. Lots of the restaurants and cafes are independent, but they do have chains like McDonald's too. Be sure to try 'pain au chocolat' for breakfast – it's delicious! Just be careful not to eat too many!

___

Although many French people understand English, it is always polite to try to speak in French. Learning the basic words like 'bonjour', 's'il vous plaît' and 'merci', isn't hard, and guide books will provide you with other useful words and expressions.

___

France is much bigger than the United Kingdom, although the number of people who live there is about the same (which is one of the reasons why the roads seem quieter). But in a country of that size, the weather can change a lot – the north is rainy just like the UK, but the south can be very, very hot in summer. In the mountains it is often snowy – it's great if you like skiing!

Watch the weather
Eating out
France – a guide for first-time visitors
Travelling in France
Learn the language

Looking at lists

■ Look at these different lists – what do they tell you about the person who wrote them?

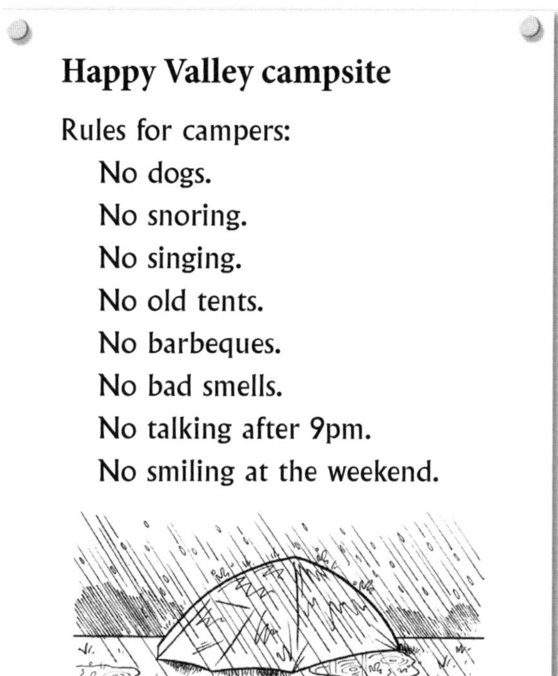

Happy Valley campsite

Rules for campers:

No dogs.
No snoring.
No singing.
No old tents.
No barbeques.
No bad smells.
No talking after 9pm.
No smiling at the weekend.

chocolate
milk
beans
chocolate
bread
potatoes
apples
chocolate

We used:
string
plastic cups
a spoon
sticky tape
a pencil

1. Set the oven to 200°C.
2. Mix sugar, butter, milk and eggs.
3. Put the mixture in a cake tin.
4. Put in the top of the oven for 20 minutes.
5. Wait for cake to cool before icing.

Organising non-narrative writing

Objective

To begin to use simple organisational devices in writing.

Background knowledge

The previous section introduced children to the terminology and use of headings, subheadings and simple lists. To move on to writing using these devices is reasonably straightforward, though as previously mentioned the tone and style of texts that are 'chunked' can be quite different from texts that rely on paragraphs. For example, there is often no continuity between sections, but the order of the sections remains very important. Also, such texts are often written in the second person as they are providing information.

Activities

- **Photocopiable page 117 'Read all about it'**
This activity encourages children to think of a heading (in this case a headline) and subheadings. The stories are already there, but without the finishing touches. Although this is similar to identifying the themes of paragraphs, it encourages the use of single words as subheadings as can happen in newspapers. To prepare, the children should have opportunities to discuss appropriate examples.
- **Photocopiable page 118 'The unfinished report'**
A strange piece of paper has been found, suspected to be from an unfinished tourist guide to planet Earth for aliens. The writer only had time to write their heading and subheadings. Can the children finish the report? You may wish to provide children with other tourist-type texts in advance, noting in particular that these are often written in the second person to make them more personal.
- **Photocopiable page 119 'Trip of a lifetime'**
This is an activity in organising and presenting information clearly. Children are asked to plan a trip and to list the things they must do and have to help plan for it. As well as introducing children to list-making, you may choose to extend this activity by asking the children to research information such as flight times and costs.

Further ideas

- **Cross-curricular thinking:** Most primary subjects provide opportunities for meaningful creation of texts, and teachers are dab-hands at doing this. For every topic covered, especially in humanities, provide opportunities for children to encounter and produce texts structured in a variety of formats. Newspapers, leaflets, encyclopedias and web pages all have their own organisational systems and attributes with which children need to become increasingly familiar.
- **List it:** The primary classroom has many opportunities for list writing, from simple inventories of materials and equipment, to sequencing instructions for PE games and activities and providing subject-related instructions. Creating and displaying such lists will enhance familiarity and understanding, as well as allowing you to introduce different formats including numbered and bulleted lists.

Digital content

On the digital component you will find:

- Printable versions of all three photocopiable pages.

Read all about it

■ This newspaper report has been written but the headline and subheadings have not been added. Your job is to come up with some eye-catching and interesting ones.

Sixty-year old Betty Stubbs couldn't believe her luck yesterday. Not only was her granddaughter Mary awarded Reader of the Year, but her cat Tiddles came home after being away for three days, then, to top it all, she won £1000 on the lottery!

A delighted Betty said, "I can't believe all these fantastic things have happened in the same day! I woke up this morning thinking about the usual jobs, but now I think I'm the luckiest person alive!"

Betty's granddaughter Mary was just as happy. "I'm so pleased that Gran has had all this good news on one day," she said. "I've always wanted to be Reader of the Year. I've worked really hard."

Betty and Mary are planning a party to celebrate. All their family and friends are being invited, and the guest of honour will probably be Tiddles!

 Name:

Organising non-narrative writing

The unfinished report

■ A strange document has been found! Believed to have been lost by aliens, it has the headings and subheadings in place for an alien tourist guide about planet Earth. Can you finish the report for the aliens?

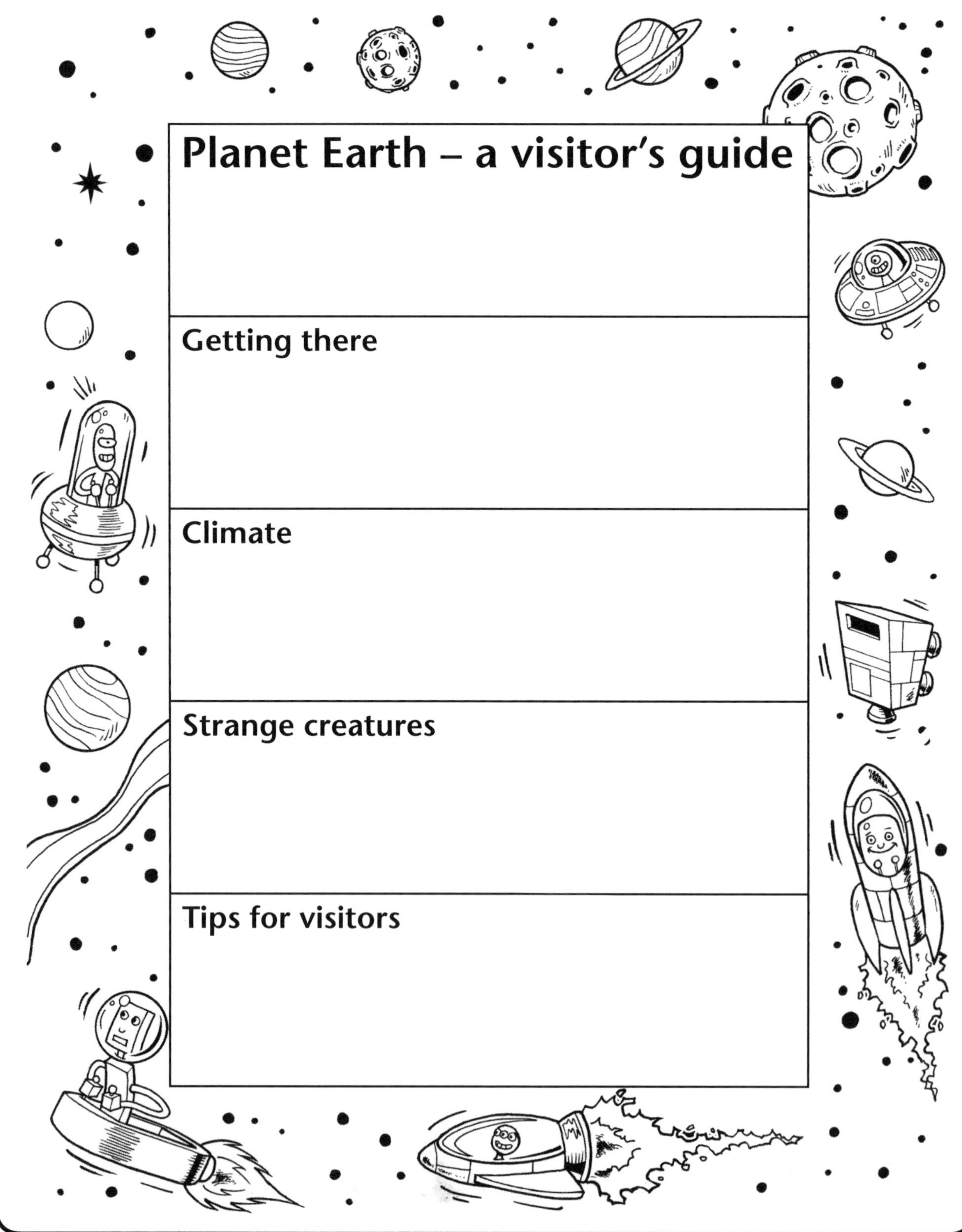

Organising non-narrative writing

Trip of a lifetime

■ Imagine that you are planning the trip of a lifetime. It is exciting but there is so much to organise! You need to make a 'to-do' list, and think about all the things you will need to take with you. Use the headings and subheadings below to help you make lists. Remember, good planning makes for great holidays!

I am going to ______________________________

Things to do now

Things to take

Clothes	Other

Things I want to do when I am on holiday

Planning and organising writing

Objective

To use paragraphs and other organisational devices in writing.

Writing focus

The activities and ideas in this section provide starting points for you to develop children's understanding and ability to organise their own writing. At this stage in their development children are often enjoying their growing ability to express themselves with pen and paper, but their thoughts can often run away with them and they can easily lapse into an almost stream-of-consciousness type of writing that can be difficult for others to decipher. The skills of paragraphing and headings can help with planning and summarising ideas and writing, and ideally should be touched on regularly and from different angles, whether reading or writing.

Skills to writing

- **Sequencing**

For new activities and knowledge presented across the curriculum, give the children prepared texts but not in order. Not only will sequencing these texts support their linguistic development, it will also enhance their understanding of the subject content.

- **Word play**

Try to have a regular display of headlines and headings from age-appropriate newspapers and/or web pages. Displaying these in isolation encourages speculation and discussion about their focus, and can lead to imaginative writing if desired.

- **Bringing skills together**

Effective paragraphs require effective sentences, and these in turn require effective word-level skills. Children's knowledge and use of clauses, punctuation and vocabulary should be maintained when crafting multi-paragraph texts.

- **Ready for dialogue?**

Although direct speech is the focus of the next chapter, at this stage you should provide support and encouragement for children who grasp the concept that a new speaker starts a new paragraph.

- **Chunk it**

As with all of their writing, children must learn strategies for self-correction and improvement. It can be rather daunting to look at a first draft and contemplate self-review and editing, and can be made much more manageable and effective by working on small chunks at a time – headings only, or perhaps the introductory paragraph.

- **Linking**

As mentioned previously, effective writing (fiction in particular) often links paragraphs carefully, even chapters. Many well-known authors, such as Michael Morpurgo, are expert at this – it is a key ingredient for creating page-turning books that are hard to put down. Highlighting the end of one paragraph and the start of the next shows how ideas carry forward while developing of changing themes are changed and developed.

Activities

- **Photocopiable page 122 'Planning stories'**

This photocopiable sheet provides a structured story-planning frame designed to encourage paragraphs in children's writing. Naturally, if children want to write longer stories, it is straightforward for them to continue the plan on the reverse.

- **Photocopiable page 123 'Organising non-fiction'**

This photocopiable sheet provides a structured planning frame designed to encourage the use of headings and subheadings to organise non-fiction writing. It will be effective when used in some of the activities suggested on the next page.

Write on

- **From screen to page**

Watch appropriate news items with the class and then work together to convert them into a newspaper article, discussing appropriate headlines and ways to break the report into sections.

- **Plan it!**

Using the writing frames on photocopiable pages 122 and 123, provide stimuli for the children to plan fiction or non-fiction texts, linked to current topics or otherwise. It is important that teachers and children evaluate and share these plans to help develop and consolidate appreciation of their importance as an integral part of effective writing.

- **Plan-swapping**

Once the children have created appropriate story plans or have listed the main headings/themes for non-fiction texts, ask them to swap and write pieces based on each other's plans. This can be an effective exercise for helping children to appreciate the importance of accuracy and conciseness in summarising paragraphs – the better they do this the fewer requests they will have for clarifications!

- **Story consequences**

Many children are familiar with the game of consequences, writing a person's name on a piece of paper, adding new sentences and then swapping these to gradually generate a funny situation. The same principle can be used for story writing, and is probably most effective with children working in similar-ability groups of around four. Guiding children with a fixed structure of your own choosing (*beginning, middle, end* is probably too simplistic at this stage) have each member of the group draft an introductory paragraph on a chosen theme before circulating their stories, continuing until all children are holding a finished draft (this might take place over several sessions). As well as developing understanding of paragraphing, the children will need to try to write in a consistent style throughout.

- **The list of lists**

Tell the class that they have been chosen as astronauts to go on a trip to Mars. They will be away for a whole year. As a class, come up with a list of all the things they need to think about taking with them: food, drink, clothes, and so on. The children can then expand these into their own lists: fruit, veg, and so on. Conclude by breaking each one down further: apples, oranges and so on. Explain that there job is to write a report for mission control presenting the information in as clear a format as possible.

Digital content

On the digital component you will find:

- Printable versions of both photocopiable pages.

Name:

Planning and organising writing

Planning stories

■ Use this writing frame to plan and organise your stories, making sure you use new paragraphs at the right times. Use the boxes to draw your paragraph themes and the lines to write the key idea for each paragraph.

Story title: ____________________

Genre: ____________________

Setting and characters: ____________________

Organising non-fiction

■ Use this writing frame to plan non-fiction reports or sets of instructions.

Heading, headline or title:	
Introduction or strapline	
Subheading 1:	
First section	
Subheading 2:	
Second section	
Subheading 3:	
Third section	
Final subheading:	
Final section or conclusion:	

Chapter 6

Apostrophes and inverted commas

Introduction

Apostrophes and inverted commas are two areas of punctuation that children can easily become confused about. This chapter provides clear examples and explanations for each aspect of punctuation followed by opportunities for practice and creative use, with a concluding section on applying these in children's own writing. For further practice, please see the 'Apostrophes an inverted commas' section of the Year 3 workbook.

Poster notes

Apostrophes (page 125)
This chart shows the rules for apostrophes for possession. As a class, collect further examples of the four different categories of the possessive apostrophe and display them on a large sheet next to the poster. Can the children spot all the nouns that are objects of possession or provide new examples?
What are they saying? (page 126)
This poster demonstrates how direct speech is presented in writing using inverted commas. It presents a small range of statements, including questions and exclamations in the familiar speech bubble format, showing their reported-speech equivalents. Create your own version of this poster based on class contributions (invented or from texts) to strengthen children's understanding.

In this chapter

Apostrophes to show possession page 127	To revisit apostrophes to mark singular possession in nouns.
Using possessive apostrophes with plurals page 131	To use apostrophes to mark plural possession in nouns.
What are they saying? page 135	To identify the words spoken by characters.
Inverted commas and direct speech page 139	To understand that in direct speech spoken words are indicated using inverted commas.
Punctuation in writing page 143	To use apostrophes and inverted commas in writing.

Vocabulary

Children should already know:
comma, apostrophe
In Year 3 children need to know:
direct speech, inverted commas (or 'speech marks')

Apostrophes and inverted commas

Apostrophes

	Noun is singular	Noun is plural
Noun doesn't end in 's'	Add apostrophe and 's' *for example: Sam in Sam's dog*	Add apostrophe and 's' *for example: children in children's dog*
Noun ends in 's'	Add apostrophe and 's' *for example: Paris in Paris's tower*	Add apostrophe *for example: babies in babies' rattles*

Apostrophes and inverted commas

What are they saying?

Using inverted commas in writing direct speech

I'm going out.

Dad said, "I'm going out."

I like swimming.

"I like swimming," said Kay.

Look out!

I shouted, "Look out!"

How old are you?

"How old are you?" asked Tina.

I'm hiding.

"I'm hiding," whispered Allan.

Stop!

"Stop!" yelled the policewoman.

Apostrophes to show possession

Objective

To revisit apostrophes to mark singular possession in nouns.

Background knowledge

Children will probably have covered the use of apostrophes for possession before, but it is a notorious area for misuse and confusion (both the location of apostrophes and their use for contractions). As such, this section aims to recap the basic facts of how apostrophes are used and what they mean.

Activities

- **Photocopiable page 128 'Reading apostrophes'**

This activity acts as a simple introduction to possessive apostrophes. Children are asked to read some sentences and examine the relationship between the word that contains the apostrophe and the word that is the object of possession.

- **Photocopiable page 129 'Our lists'**

This activity involves children in the task of making lists of phrases that include apostrophes. Initially, work though the examples with the class (in particular pointing out James's yo-yo, reinforcing the 's's' construction for names ending in 's').

- **Photocopiable page 130 'Contraction or possession?'**

Children must decide whether the apostrophe in each sentence has a role of contraction or possession. You will need to consider how much attention to pay to reviewing contractions prior to this lesson. Clearly displaying these rules may be beneficial too. Remember that apostrophes show where two words have been brought together and one or more letters removed – for example 'didn't' – with the apostrophe marking the place where the letter has been removed, not where the words are joined.

Further ideas

- **Everything I own:** Either print a picture of a character or draw one, and then draw a range of everyday possessions around the character. Then label each item, for example *Henry's saucepan*.
- **Examining examples:** When children find examples of apostrophes used to indicate possession in their reading, encourage them to use photocopiable page 128 'Reading apostrophes' to examine the relationship between the word with the apostrophe and the noun to which it belongs.
- **Expand it:** Whether focusing on apostrophes for possession or contraction, provide the children with small texts including such examples, then ask them to highlight them and write the 'meaning' (for example, *the sword of Bilbo, it did not matter*) at the side.

Digital content

On the digital component you will find:

- Printable versions of all three photocopiable pages.
- Answers to 'Reading apostrophes' and 'Contraction or possession?'.
- Interactive versions of 'Reading apostrophes' and 'Contraction or possession?'.

Name:

Apostrophes to show possession

Reading apostrophes

■ Look at these sentences. In each there is a word with a possessive apostrophe. Something belongs to the noun that ends with the apostrophe.

Look at Sam's dog.

The apostrophe shows:

The dog belongs to Sam.

■ Complete the sentences, showing who or what 'possesses' something.

Sophie's bike is really fast.

The ________________ belongs to ________________.

Mr Hall mended the cat's collar.

The ________________ belongs to ________________.

The teacher found the boy's shoe.

The ________________ belongs to ________________.

We found a stripy snail's shell.

The ________________ belongs to ________________.

Everyone waited for the orchestra's conductor.

The ________________ belongs to ________________.

The farmer put the cow's food in the trough.

The ________________ belongs to ________________.

After school, Micah and Louie went to Toby's house.

The ________________ belongs to ________________.

Apostrophes to show possession

Our lists

■ Jamie asked eight children in his class: 'What is your favourite toy?' He recorded the results using apostrophes to show who said what.

Tracy's football
Kirpan's magic set
Caroline's troll
Jan's train set
Harry's space rider
Tara's chemistry set
James's yo-yo
Nathan's computer game

■ Ask children in your class each question and make a list under each heading. Remember to use the apostrophe.

Best toy	**Clothing**	**Relative who gets the most visits**
Which toy is your absolute favourite?	What's your favourite item of clothing?	Which of your relatives do you visit the most?

Name:

Apostrophes to show possession

Contraction or possession?

■ Look at the sentences. Sort them into two groups. Put a 'P' in the box for a sentence that has an apostrophe of possession. Put a 'C' in the box for a sentence that has an apostrophe of contraction. The words have been circled to help you.

The farmer sheared the sheep's wool. ☐

Chris's family come from Scotland. ☐

Don't put too much food in the fish tank. ☐

I think I'll go to the park after school. ☐

The cook made the children's dinners. ☐

My class hasn't done PE this week. ☐

On Mum's birthday we made her a cake. ☐

My grandpa said he'd meet me after school. ☐

Some people are painting the doctor's surgery. ☐

Jane walked to her friend's house. ☐

The washing machine didn't work. ☐

They watched the film on Gail's television. ☐

Using possessive apostrophes with plurals

Objective

To use apostrophes to mark plural possession in nouns.

Background knowledge

Children should now know that apostrophes can be used to show possession. An apostrophe in a word that is a noun can show it possesses a following item (for example, *Sean's book*). Rules for adding apostrophes depend on the nouns to which they are being added. As shown on the poster on page 125, singular nouns add 'apostrophe s' no matter what letter they end in (for example *dog's bone*, *Paris's restaurants*).

However, care must be taken with plural nouns: if they do not end in 's' they take 'apostrophe s' as usual (for example *children's books*, *mice's food*) but if they do end in 's' the only take an apostrophe (for example *babies' toys*, *teachers' car park*).

Activities

- **Photocopiable page 132 'It belongs to them'**
This activity gently focuses children's learning on the use of possessive apostrophes with plural nouns, asking them to match the long and short form of possessive statements. There are examples of plurals ending in 's', and others that do not. None of the sentences need to be corrected or altered. In reviewing children's work be sure to provide opportunities for them to read all of the sentences aloud.
- **Photocopiable page 133 'Using possessive apostrophes in plurals'**
Children are now asked to insert apostrophes into a text containing a range of plural nouns. The text is quite straightforward and contains no singular nouns requiring possessive apostrophes. However, the children will need to remember the basic rule that a second 's' is not required and that possessive apostrophes come at the end of plurals with an 's'.
- **Photocopiable page 134 'Singular and plural'**
In this activity children encounter the various rules for adding apostrophes of possession to nouns. They then try a set of examples. The two crucial questions about the noun are: *Is it singular or plural?* and *Does it end in the letter 's'?* (See poster page 125.)

Further ideas

- **Examples:** Provide the children with reading material in which they can find examples of the possessive apostrophe that cover each of the rules. Can they think of their own examples of phrases that use apostrophes for possession? Suggest that they compile examples inspired by characters from books or television.
- **Our school:** Think about the school and make possessive statements about things that belong to the children and the teachers. For example, *the teachers' car park*, *the children's play equipment*, and so on.
- **Redrafting:** Ask the children to review pieces of their own writing, finding points at which they could have used apostrophes.

Digital content

On the digital component you will find:

- Printable versions of all three photocopiable pages.
- Answers to all three photocopiable pages.
- Interactive version of 'Using possessive apostrophes in plurals'.

Name:

Using possessive apostrophes with plurals

It belongs to them

■ Match the sentences on the left to the ones on the right. Look at how the sentences on the right use possessive apostrophes for plural nouns.

That dog belongs to the children.	It is the sparrows' nest.
That cheese is for the mice.	It is the children's dog.
These horses live in this stable.	It is the women's house.
Three women own that house.	It is the badgers' burrow.
This nest belongs to those sparrows.	They are these trees' leaves.
The badgers are in their burrow.	They are the families' caravans.
The leaves fell off these trees.	It is the horses' stable.
The caravans belong to those families.	It is the mice's cheese.

Using possessive apostrophes in plurals

■ Look at the following passage. There are ten plural nouns with their possessive apostrophes removed. The words have been underlined. Can you put the apostrophes in the correct place?

The Wilson family live on Bluebell farm. Their life is very busy. Everyone gets up at six o'clock in the morning. Mr Wilson makes the <u>childrens</u> porridge while Mrs Wilson goes to the <u>chickens</u> shed and collects eggs. The <u>eggs</u> shells are golden-brown.

The <u>childrens</u> school is miles away and they have to catch a bus. Once they have gone, Mr and Mrs Wilson prepare the <u>animals</u> food. Then Mr Wilson visits the <u>pigs</u> field and Mrs Wilson goes to the <u>cows</u> barn to feed the animals and check they are well.

It isn't just cows that live in the barn, there are two nests – in the roof is a <u>swallows</u> nest, and in a corner behind a pile of hay there is a tiny <u>mices</u> nest.

In the evenings all the animals curl up snug in their beds, and so do the children! But their <u>parents</u> jobs are still not finished – they have to check that all the doors are locked and all the dishes are washed, ready for another day.

Name:

Using possessive apostrophes with plurals

Singular and plural

Where you place an apostrophe depends on the word it is added to.

The owner	The rule	Examples
is singular, doesn't end in 's'	add an apostrophe and 's'	*Sam's dog* *Lisa's football*
is singular, ends in 's'	add an apostrophe and 's'	*Ross's cat* *Paris's tower*
is plural, doesn't end in 's'	add an apostrophe and 's'	*the children's dog* *the mice's nest*
is plural, ends in 's'	add an apostrophe only (no 's')	*the babies' rattles* *the teachers' mugs*

Look at this sentence.

The bike belongs to Pete.

Turn it into a phrase that has an apostrophe. It becomes:

Pete's bike

Look at the thing or person who owns. Is there one or more? Does the word end in 's'?

■ Turn these sentences into phrases that have apostrophes.

The football belongs to Kate. ______________________

The quiz game belongs to the class. ______________________

The playground belongs to the children. ______________________

The mugs belong to the teachers. ______________________

The lids belong to the boxes. ______________________

The houses belong to the people. ______________________

The farm belongs to the women. ______________________

The driver belongs to the bus. ______________________

The cat belongs to Ross. ______________________

What are they saying?

Objective

To identify the words spoken by characters.

Background knowledge

Children should understand that inverted commas separate speech from the rest of the sentence. At this stage, they are not asked to use them – only to be aware of their function. Use Big Books or digital texts to look at this. Children might underline a character's words and/or circle the speech marks.

Activities

- **Photocopiable page 136 'Write the answers'**
Show the children that there are five situations on the sheet, and in each case there are two children. The children should read the words spoken by the child on the left and decide what the child on the right might reply, writing the words in the speech bubble.
- **Photocopiable page 137 'Suzie and the spider'**
Explain to the children that Mrs Dray is a busy squirrel with a young family whose demands take up a lot of her time. Today, she wants some time to herself. Read the extract together before asking the children to re-read it to themselves, looking for the words that the squirrels speak. Tell them to shade the spoken words lightly with a coloured pencil. They can then read it aloud in pairs, talking about how the squirrels might have said the words.
- **Photocopiable page 138 'Speech shading'**
In this activity, the children identify speech in texts. The texts for this activity are taken from: *Farmer Duck* by Martin Waddell (Walker Books); the meeting of Eddie and the Bear, each carrying the other's teddy in *Where's My Teddy?* by Jez Alborough (Walker Books); the conversation among the owls left alone from *Owl Babies* by Martin Waddell (Walker Books). Re-writing the texts using inverted commas is a logical next step if time permits.

Further ideas

- **Writing spoken words:** Display several photographs of different people and attach a large paper speech bubble to each person. Ask the children to suggest what each person might be saying. Agree some words for the first and write them in the bubble. Draw attention to the fact that you don't write 'he said' or 'she shouted', only the spoken words.
- **Identifying dialogue:** In shared reading, focus on an extract from a familiar story that has plenty of dialogue. Read the extract, telling the children to look carefully for the words that the characters speak. Children might take on the roles of the characters and act out the conversation, saying only the words of the appropriate character. A follow-on exercise might be to present the dialogue as a cartoon strip with speech bubbles.
- **Acting:** Invite pairs of children to act out the story on photocopiable page 137 'Suzie and the spider', taking on the roles of Suzie and Mrs Dray. Emphasise that they must say only the words that were spoken by the characters. Again, this might be presented subsequently as a cartoon strip

Digital content

On the digital component you will find:

- Printable versions of all three photocopiable pages.
- Answers to 'Suzie the spider' and 'Speech shading'.
- Interactive version of 'Suzie and the spider'.

Name:

What are they saying?

Write the answers

■ Read what each child says. What do you think the other child answers?

What are they saying?

Suzie and the spider

■ Shade the words that are spoken.

"What are you doing, Suzie?" asked Mrs Dray.

"I'm watching that spider," said Suzie, smiling.

"Spider! Where?" her mum gasped.

"It's gone under the table," replied Suzie. "I can't see it any more."

Mrs Dray didn't like spiders, but was not going to look for it now. She looked at Suzie and said, "You're meant to be helping Dad look after the baby."

"Yes," muttered Suzie. But she didn't move.

"Off you go, then," Mrs Dray said. "I'm going to sit here quietly. And I don't want to be disturbed."

■ What do you think happened next? Did the spider come back? What did Mum say? What about Dad?

Name:

What are they saying?

Speech shading

- Look at these passages from stories. Some of these words were said by characters in the story. For example, in

The duck answered, "Quack!" the duck said the word, Quack.

- Using a colouring pencil, gently shade over the words that were actually spoken.

The duck awoke and waddled wearily into the yard
expecting to hear, How goes the work?
But nobody spoke!
Then the cow and the sheep and the hens came back.
Quack? asked the duck.
Moo! said the cow.
Baa! said the sheep.
Cluck! said the hens.
Which told the duck the whole story.

from *Farmer Duck* by Martin Waddell

MY TED! gasped the bear.
A BEAR! screamed Eddy.
A BOY! yelled the bear.
MY TEDDY! cried Eddy.

from *Where's My Teddy?* by Jez Alborough

One night they woke up and their owl mother was GONE.
Where's Mummy? asked Sarah.
Oh my goodness! said Percy.
I want my Mummy! said Bill.
The baby owls thought
(all owls think a lot) –
I think she's gone hunting, said Sarah.
To get us our food! said Percy.
I want my Mummy! said Bill.

from *Owl Babies* by Martin Waddell

Inverted commas and direct speech

Objective

To understand that in direct speech spoken words are indicated using inverted commas.

Background knowledge

Inverted commas are sometimes referred to as speech marks. They are used to demarcate the words that were actually spoken in a sentence. In a sentence like *Mum said, "Tidy up"* the inverted commas enclose the words that Mum actually said. Lines of speech can be separated from the words denoting who is speaking in three ways:

The speech can come after the other words: *Mum said, "Can you lot go and tidy your room?"*

Or before them: *"Can you lot go and tidy your room?" Mum said.*

Or the speech can be separated by other words: *"Can you lot go," Mum said, "and tidy your room."*

In each of these, the inverted commas enclose the actual words spoken. Note also how other punctuation is used within inverted commas, and how commas are usually used to mark the gap between a set of words that are spoken and other words.

Activities

- **Photocopiable page 140 'Marking out speech'**
As they read the poem 'Overheard on a Saltmarsh', the children can try figuring out which of the two speakers is saying the individual lines. This activity can act as a prelude to other reading activities. The piece can be read by two groups taking the parts of the two characters, or you can read one part and the children respond with the other.
- **Photocopiable page 141 'Direct speech'**
Children convert a dialogue with speech bubbles to direct speech using speech marks. By remodelling the scripted passage as dialogue, they get experience of trying a range of words to describe the act of speaking. If appropriate the conversation could be extended using children's own ideas.
- **Photocopiable page 142 'Bubble time'**
This activity continues to familiarise children with direct speech and the punctuation within it. A selection of brief dialogue exchanges are presented, and children's task is to present these in cartoon format using speech bubbles, ensuring they use the appropriate punctuation – capital letters and full-stops (not commas), exclamation marks or question marks.

Further ideas

- **Carpet talk:** During class discussions, explain to the class that, over the coming week, you are occasionally going to stop a speaker after they have said something and ask the class to figure out how that act of speaking would be recorded in an account of the event written later on. For the next week, every so often, after a child has said something like *Can I take the register downstairs?* stop the class and ask them to model the event as a sentence on the board (for example: *Fozia asked, "Can I take the register downstairs?"*).
- **Dialogue:** Ask the children to find passages in novels in which a group of characters are speaking and try acting out the passage, each taking a role and saying aloud the words ascribed to that character. Point out to the class that they can find the lines for their drama by looking for the spoken words demarcated in the text.

Digital content

On the digital component you will find:

- Printable versions of all three photocopiable pages.
- Answers to 'Marking out speech'.

Name:

Inverted commas and direct speech

Marking out speech

- There are two speakers in this poem – a nymph and a goblin. Read the poem carefully.
- Can you work out which lines the goblin is saying? Can you work out which lines the nymph is saying?
- Shade over the nymph's lines in one colour and the goblin's lines in another.

Overheard on a Saltmarsh

Nymph, nymph, what are your beads?
Green glass, goblin. Why do you stare at them?
Give them me.
No.
Give them me. Give them me.
No.
Then I will howl all night in the reeds,
Lie in the mud and howl for them.

Goblin, why do you love them so?

They are better than stars or water,
Better than voices of winds that sing,
Better than any man's fair daughter,
Your green glass beads on a silver ring.

Hush, I stole them out of the moon.

Give my your beads, I want them.
No.
I will howl in a deep lagoon
For your green glass beads, I love them so.
Give them me. Give them me.
No.

Harold Monro

SCHOLASTIC
www.scholastic.co.uk

Name:

Inverted commas and direct speech

Direct speech

■ Look at the conversation below.

■ Turn over this sheet and rewrite the conversation as a passage with direct speech. A start has been made for you here.

"Wake up. It's time for school," said Lou.

"I don't want to go to school," grumbled Sam.

Name:

Inverted commas and direct speech

Bubble time

■ Read each of the short conversations below, and then create a small cartoon for each one with a speech bubble for each character.

Tip: Do not draw the bubble until you have written the words that will go inside it.

<table>
<tr>
<td>"The film is starting," said Josie.
"Quick, turn your mobile off," replied her mum.
</td>
<td>"Go and tidy your room!" yelled his dad.
"I don't want to," moaned Tim.
</td>
</tr>
<tr>
<td>"Where is your homework?" demanded the teacher.
"Err, the dog ate it," replied Tamsin.
 </td>
<td>"We are going to do art all day," said the teacher.
"Yessssssss!" shouted the class.
</td>
</tr>
</table>

Punctuation in writing

Objective

To use apostrophes and inverted commas in writing.

Writing focus

Building on previous activities on apostrophes and inverted commas, this section encourages children to apply their knowledge of punctuation to their own writing.

Skills to writing

- **Apostrophe spotting**

The best resource for encouraging children to use punctuation in their own writing is to see it in use, briefly and often, in common texts. Keep on the lookout for apostrophes and, as they are found, deconstruct them. Are they used to show possession or contraction? If the former, who possesses what, and which rule has been applied? If the latter, what has been omitted?

- **Checking apostrophes**

Apostrophes provide a useful focus for redrafting activities. At this age apostrophes are easily left out or misapplied. Ask the children to revisit some previous pieces of writing with a view to identifying any revisions they could make. Moving beyond their written work, encourage the children to look in the wider environment and at other printed texts for examples of apostrophe omission or error. It's a common one – so they should find a few!

- **Sentence by sentence**

In the first stages of Key Stage 2, teaching should still be very focused on securing punctuated sentences. All other punctuation marks flow from an understanding of the demarcated sentence. As the children are writing, make sure they think sentence by sentence. Use that idea in shared, modelled and guided writing.

- **Writing speech**

Take every opportunity for writing speech. When writing news stories and non-fiction recounts, encourage children to put in and demarcate the speech of the participants. Every recount should be coupled with the question: *Who said what?*

- **Revision**

Revisit writing to find the places where punctuation has been missed. Children can work in writing trios, where each child reads the writing of their teammates and particularly checks for punctuation possibilities and errors.

Activities

- **Photocopiable page 145 'Whose what?'**

This activity helps to reinforce the concept of possessive apostrophes. Children must assign objects to different people and write simple sentences using possessive apostrophes. This can be extended by using the construction in more complex sentences, or indeed by comparing people's objects, such as *Peter's pen is newer than Zara's pencil.*

- **Photocopiable page 146 'Speech bubbles'**

The bubbles on the photocopiable sheet can be used to stimulate the devising of conversations. The model can be used in shared or guided writing. Children can contribute their thoughts about what participants say in the exchange, but once notes have been made they can then take this and write up the conversation in punctuated reported speech.

Write on

- **Possession poems**

Ask the class to devise some list poems that tell us something about the possessions of well-known figure. Take the birthday parties of certain characters. What would they be like?

At Dracula's birthday party they…

At Captain Hook's birthday party they…

Finish the lines and add some more to create a list poem that catalogues insights into favourite characters.

- **Annotated maps**

When reading stories set in particular places and in discussion with the class, create a map of the locality (whether a house, an island or a town), and label the map showing the habitats of different characters, such as *Gollum's cave*, *Tracey's house*, *Red Riding Hood's cottage*, and so on, emphasising the possessive apostrophes. This can be extended to drawing and labelling significant objects from the story, such as *Bilbo's ring*, *Rapunzel's hair*, *Timmy's collar*, and so on. The children can then be challenged to write a sentence for each item.

- **Conversation acting**

To stimulate the writing of good speech, encourage the children to act out exchanges in any text they may be writing. For example, working in twos, they can play out the argument two characters in a story might have. They don't need to rewrite the conversation word for word – far better that they listen out for and deploy the best lines in their text.

- **Equip characters**

Together, devise characters for an adventure story and kit them out with the possessions they will take on their adventures. Whether it's *Tim's rope-ladder* or *Imogen's parachute*, the children can decide why that character needs that item. Point out that a character is never kitted out with something they won't use at some point in the story. The gadget, the spell, and the piece of junk they found – they all come in useful at some point in the plot.

Digital content

On the digital component you will find:

- Printable versions of both photocopiable pages.

Name:

Whose what?

■ Match a person to an object and write a sentence using a possessive apostrophe.

For example: *Peter's pen is blue.*

Name:

Punctuation in writing

Speech bubbles

■ Use the speech bubbles to draft a conversation between two characters.

Subject knowledge

1. Preliminary notes about grammar

Grammar involves the way in which words of different types are combined into sentences. The explanatory sections that follow will include definitions of types of word along with notes on how they are combined into sentences.

Three preliminary points about grammar:

- Function is all-important. Where a word is placed in relation to another word is crucial in deciding whether it is functioning as a verb or a noun. For example, the word 'run' will often be thought of as a verb. However, in a sentence like *They went for a run*, the word functions as a noun and the verb is 'went'.
- There are some consistencies in the way spelling is linked to grammar. For example, words like 'play' and 'shout' have the 'ed' ending to make past tense verbs, 'played' and 'shouted'. Adjectives like 'quick' and 'slow' take a 'ly' ending to make adverbs like 'quickly' and 'slowly'. There are exceptions to these rules but such consistencies can still prove useful when it comes to understanding the grammar of sentences.
- Nothing is sacred in language. Rules change over time; the double negative has gained currency, and regional variation in accent and dialect is now far more valued than has been the case in the past. The rules of grammar that follow are subject to change as the language we use lives and grows.

2. Words and functions

Grammar picks out the functions of words. The major classes or types of word in the English language are:

Noun

The name of something or someone, including concrete things, such as 'dog' or 'tree', and abstract things, such as 'happiness' or 'fear'.

Pronoun

A word that replaces a noun. The noun 'John' in *John is ill* can be replaced by a pronoun 'he', making *He is ill*.

Verb

A word that denotes an action or a happening. In the sentence *I ate the cake* the verb is 'ate'. These are sometimes referred to as 'doing' words.

Adjective

A word that modifies a noun. In the phrase *the little boat* the adjective 'little' describes the noun 'boat'.

Adverb
A word that modifies a verb. In the phrase *he slowly walked* the adverb is 'slowly'.

Preposition
A word or phrase that shows the relationship of one thing to another. In the phrase *the house beside the sea* the preposition 'beside' places the two nouns in relation to each other.

Conjunction
A word or phrase that joins other words and phrases. A simple example is the word 'and' that joins nouns in *Snow White and Doc and Sneezy*.

Determiner
Determiners appear before nouns and denote whether the noun is specific (*give me the book*) or not (*give me a book*). Note that 'the' (definite article) and 'a' or 'an' (indefinite articles) are the most common types of determiner.

Interjection
A word or phrase expressing or exclaiming an emotion, such as 'Oh!' and 'Aaargh!'
The various word types can be found in the following example sentences:

Lou	saw	his	new	house	from	the	train.
noun	verb	pronoun	adjective	noun	preposition	article	noun
Yeow!	I	hit	my	head	on	the	door.
interjection	pronoun	verb	pronoun	noun	preposition	article	noun
Amir	sadly	lost	his	bus fare	down	the	drain.
noun	adverb	verb	pronoun	noun	preposition	article	noun
Give	Jan	a	good	book	for	her	birthday.
verb	noun	article	adjective	noun	conjunction	pronoun	noun

The pages that follow provide more information on these word classes.

Nouns

There are four types of noun in English.

A **noun** is the name of someone or something.

Common nouns are general names for things. For example, in the sentence *I fed the dog*, the noun 'dog' could be used to refer to any dog, not to a specific one. Other examples include 'boy', 'country', 'book', 'apple'.

Proper nouns are the specific names given to identify things or people. In a phrase like *Sam is my dog* the word 'dog' is the common noun but 'Sam' is a proper noun because it refers to and identifies a specific dog. Other examples include 'Wales' and 'Amazing Grace'.

Collective nouns refer to a group of things together, such as 'a flock (of sheep)' or 'a bunch (of bananas)'.

Abstract nouns refer to things that are not concrete, such as an action, a concept, an event, quality or state. Abstract nouns like 'happiness' and 'fulfilment' refer to ideas or feelings which are non-countable; others, such as 'hour', 'joke' and 'quantity' are countable.

Nouns can be singular or plural. To change a singular to a plural the usual rule is to add 's'. This table includes other rules to bear in mind:

If the singular ends in:	Rule	Examples
'y' after a consonant	Remove 'y', add 'ies'	party → parties
'y' after a vowel	add 's'	donkey → donkeys
'o' after a consonant	add 'es'	potato → potatoes
'o' after a vowel	add 's'	video → videos
an 's' sound such as 's', 'sh', 'x', 'z'	add 'es'	kiss → kisses dish → dishes
a 'ch' sound such as 'ch' or 'tch'	add 'es'	watch → watches church → churches

Pronouns

There are different classes of pronoun. These are the main types:

A **pronoun** is a word that stands in for a noun.

Personal pronouns refer to people or things, such as 'I', 'you', 'it'. The personal pronouns distinguish between subject and object case ('I/me', 'he/him', 'she/her', 'we/us', 'they/them' and the archaic 'thou/thee').

Reflexive pronouns refer to people or things that are also the subject of the sentence. In the sentence *You can do this yourself* the pronoun 'yourself' refers to 'you'. Such pronouns end with 'self' or 'selves'. Other examples include 'myself', 'themselves'.

Possessive pronouns identify people or things as belonging to a person or thing. For example, in the sentence *The book is hers* the possessive pronoun 'hers' refers to 'the book'. Other examples include 'its' and 'yours'. Note that possessive pronouns never take an apostrophe.

Relative pronouns link relative clauses to their nouns. In the sentence *The man who was in disguise sneaked into the room* the relative clause 'who was in disguise' provides extra information about 'the man'. This relative clause is linked by the relative pronoun 'who'. Other examples include 'whom', 'which' and 'that'.

Interrogative pronouns are used in questions. They refer to the thing that is being asked about. In the question *What is your name?* and *Where is the book?* the pronouns 'what' and 'where' stand for the answers – the name and the location of the book.

Demonstrative pronouns are pronouns that 'point'. They are used to show the relation of the speaker to an object. There are four demonstrative pronouns in English 'this', 'that', 'these', 'those' used as in *This is my house* and *That is your house*. They have specific uses, depending upon the position of the object to the speaker:

	Near to speaker	**Far away from speaker**
Singular	this	that
Plural	these	those

Indefinite pronouns stand in for an indefinite noun. The indefinite element can be the number of elements or the nature of them but they are summed up in ambiguous pronouns such as 'any', 'some' or 'several'. Other examples are the pronouns that end with 'body', 'one' and 'thing', such as 'somebody', 'everyone' and 'anything'.

Person

Personal, reflexive and possessive pronouns can be in the first, second or third person.

- First-person pronouns ('I', 'we') involve the speaker or writer.
- Second-person pronouns ('you') refer to the listener or reader.
- Third-person pronouns refer to something other than these two participants in the communication ('he', 'she', 'it', 'they').

The person of the pronoun will agree with particular forms of verbs: 'I like'/'she likes'.

Verbs

The **tense** of a verb places a happening in time. The main tenses are the present and past.

English does not have a discrete future tense. It is made in a compound form using a present tense ('I will', 'I shall' and so on) and an infinitive (for example *I will go to the shops*).

The regular past tense is formed by the addition of the suffix 'ed', although some of the most common verbs in English have irregular past tenses.

A **verb** is a word that denotes an action or a happening.

Present tense (happening now)	**Past tense (happened in past)**	**Future (to happen in future)**
am, say, find, kick	was, said, found, kicked	will be, will say, shall find, shall kick

Continuous verbs

The present participle form of a verb is used to show a continuous action. Whereas a past tense like 'kicked' denotes an action that happened ('I kicked'), the present participle denotes the action as happening and continuing as it is described (*I was kicking*, the imperfect tense, or *I am kicking*, the present continuous). There is a sense in these uses of an action that has not ended.

The present participle usually ends in 'ing', such as 'walking', 'finding', and continuous verbs are made with a form of the verb 'be', such as 'was' or 'am': *I was running* and *I am running*.

Auxiliary verbs

Auxiliary verbs 'help' other verbs – they regularly accompany full verbs, always preceding them in a verb phrase. The auxiliary verbs in English can be divided into three categories:

Primary verbs are used to indicate the timing of a verb, such as 'be', 'have' or 'did' (including all their variations such as 'was', 'were', 'has', 'had' and so on). These can be seen at work in verb forms like *I was watching a film, He has finished eating, I didn't lose my keys*.

Modal verbs indicate the possibility of an action occurring or the necessity of it happening, such as *I might watch a film*, *I should finish eating* and *I shouldn't lose my keys*.

The modal verbs in English are: 'would', 'could', 'might', 'should', 'can', 'will', 'shall', 'may', and 'must'. These verbs never function on their own as main verbs. They always act as auxiliaries helping other verbs.

Marginal modals, namely 'dare', 'need', 'ought to' and 'used to'. These act as modals, such as in the sentences *I dared enter the room*, *You need to go away* and *I ought to eat my dinner*, but they can also act as main verbs, as in *I need cake*.

Adjectives

An **adjective** is a word that modifies a noun.

The main function of adjectives is to define quality or quantity. Examples of the use of descriptions of quality include 'good story', 'sad day' and 'stupid dog'. Examples of the use of descriptions of quantity include 'some stories', 'ten days' and 'many dogs'.

Adjectives can appear in one of three different degrees of intensity. In the table below it can be seen that there are 'er' and 'est' endings that show an adjective is comparative or superlative, though, there are exceptions. The regular comparative is formed by the addition of the suffix 'er' to shorter words and 'more' to longer words ('kind/kinder', 'beautiful/more beautiful'). The regular superlative is formed by the addition of the suffix 'est' to shorter words and 'most' to longer words. Note, however, that some common adjectives are irregular.

Nominative The nominative is the plain form that describes a noun.	**Comparative** The comparative implies a comparison between the noun and something else.	**Superlative** The superlative is the ultimate degree of a particular quality.
Examples	**Examples**	**Examples**
long	longer	longest
small	smaller	smallest
big	bigger	biggest
fast	faster	fastest
bad	worse	worst
good	better	best
far	farther/further	farthest/furthest

Adverbs

Adverbs provide extra information about the time, place or manner in which the action of a verb happened.

An **adverb** is a word that modifies a verb.

Manner Provides information about the manner in which the action was done.	Ali *quickly* ran home. The cat climbed *fearfully* up the tree.
Time Provides information about the time at which the action occurred.	*Yesterday* Ali ran home. *Sometimes* the cat climbed up the tree.
Place Provides information about where the action took place.	*Outside* Ali ran home. *In the garden* the cat climbed up the tree.

Variations in the degree of intensity of an adverb are indicated by other adjectives such as 'very', 'rather', 'quite' and 'somewhat'. Comparative forms include 'very quickly', 'rather slowly', and 'most happily'.

The majority of single-word adverbs are made by adding 'ly' to an adjective: 'quick/quickly', 'slow/slowly' and so on.

Prepositions

Prepositions show how nouns or pronouns are positioned in relation to other nouns and pronouns in the same sentence. This can often be the location of one thing in relation to another in space, such as 'on', 'over', 'near'; or time, such as 'before', 'after'.

Prepositions are usually placed before a noun. They can consist of one word (*The cat* in *the tree...*), two words (*The cat* close to *the gate...*) or three (*The cat* on top of *the roof...*).

A **preposition** is a word or phrase that shows the relationship of one thing to another.

Determiners

There are different types of determiner:

A **determiner** identifies whether a noun is known or unknown.

Articles are the most common type: 'the' (definite article) and 'a' or 'an' (indefinite article).

Possessives are often possessive pronouns such as 'my', 'your', 'our', but can also be nouns with an apostrophe, with or without an 's' (as in *Jane's car, the Prime Minister's speech, the girls' results*.)

Demonstratives are used to show the relation of the speaker to an object. There are four demonstrative pronouns in English 'this', 'that', 'these', 'those'. (See page 150.)

Quantifiers are used to express the quantity of a noun, for example: (indefinite quantity) 'some', 'many', 'several'; (definite quantity) 'every', 'both', 'all', 'four', 'seventy'.

Connectives

The job of a connective is to maintain cohesion through a piece of text.

A **connective** is a word or phrase that links clauses or sentences.

Connectives can be:

- Conjunctions – connect clauses within one sentence.
- Connecting adverbs – connect ideas in separate sentences.

Conjunctions

Conjunctions are a special type of connective. There are two types: coordinating and subordinating.

Coordinating conjunctions connect clauses of equal weight. For example: *I like cake and I like tea.* Coordinating conjunctions include: 'and', 'but', 'or' and 'so'.

Subordinating conjunctions are used where the clauses of unequal weight, they begin a subordinate clause. For example: *The dog barked because he saw the burglar.* Subordinating conjunctions include: 'because', 'when', 'while', 'that', 'although', 'if', 'until', 'after', before' and 'since'.

Name of conjunction	Nature of conjunction	Examples
Addition	One or more clause together	We had our tea *and* went out to play.
Opposition	One or more clauses in opposition	I like coffee *but* my brother hates it. It could rain *or* it could snow.
Time	One or more clauses connected over time	Toby had his tea *then* went out to play. The bus left *before* we reached the stop.
Cause	One or more clauses causing or caused by another	I took a map *so that* we wouldn't get lost. We got lost *because* we had the wrong map.

Connecting adverbs

The table below provides the function of the adverbs and examples of the type of words used for that purpose.

Addition	'also', 'furthermore', 'moreover', 'likewise'
Opposition	'however', 'never the less', 'on the other hand'
Time	'just then', 'meanwhile', 'later'
Result	'therefore', 'as a result'
Reinforcing	'besides', 'anyway'
Explaining	'for example', 'in other words'
Listing	'first of all', 'finally'

3. Understanding sentences

Types of sentence

The four main types of sentence are declarative, interrogative, imperative and exclamatory. The function of a sentence has an effect on the word order; imperatives, for example, often begin with a verb.

Sentence type	Function	Examples
Declarative	Makes a statement	The house is down the lane. Joe rode the bike.
Interrogative	Asks a question	Where is the house? What is Joe doing?
Imperative	Issues a command or direction	Turn left at the traffic lights. Get on your bike!
Exclamatory	Issues an interjection	Wow, what a mess! Oh no!

Sentences: Clauses and complexities

Phrases

A phrase is a set of words performing a grammatical function. In the sentence *The little, old, fierce dog brutally chased the sad and fearful cat*, there are three distinct units performing grammatical functions. The first phrase in this sentence essentially names the dog and provides descriptive information. This is a noun phrase, performing the job of a noun – 'the little, old, fierce dog'. To do this the phrase uses adjectives.

The important thing to look out for is the way in which words build around a key word in a phrase. So here the words 'little', 'old' and 'fierce' are built around the word 'dog'. In examples like these, 'dog' is referred to as the **headword** and the adjectives are termed **modifiers**. Together, the modifier and headword make up the noun phrase. Modifiers can also come after the noun, as in *The little, old, fierce dog that didn't like cats brutally chased the sad and fearful cat*. In this example 'little, 'old' and 'fierce' are **premodifiers** and the phrase 'that didn't like cats' is a **postmodifier**. The noun phrase is just one of the types of phrase that can be made.

Phrase type	Examples
Noun phrase	The *little, old fierce dog* didn't like cats. She gave him *a carefully and colourfully covered book*.
Verb phrase	The dog *had been hiding* in the house. The man *climbed through* the window without a sound.
Adjectival phrase	The floor was *completely clean*. The floor was *so clean you could eat your dinner off it*.
Adverbial phrase	I finished my lunch *very slowly indeed*. *More confidently than usual*, she entered the room.
Prepositional phrase	The cat sat *at the top of* the tree. The phone rang *in the middle of* the night.

Notice that phrases can appear within phrases. A noun phrase like 'carefully and colourfully covered book' contains the adjectival phrase 'carefully and colourfully covered'. This string of words forms the adjectival phrase in which the words 'carefully' and 'colourfully' modify the adjective 'covered'. Together these words, 'carefully and colourfully covered', modify the noun 'book', creating a distinct noun phrase. This is worth noting as it shows how the boundaries between phrases can be blurred – a fact that can cause confusion unless borne in mind!

Clauses

Clauses are units of meaning included within a sentence, usually containing a verb and other elements linked to it. *The burglar ran* is a clause containing the definite article, noun and verb; *The burglar quickly ran from the little house* is also a clause that adds an adverb, preposition and adjective. The essential element in a clause is the verb. Clauses look very much like small sentences – indeed sentences can be constructed of just one clause: *The burglar hid*, *I like cake*.

Sentences can also be constructed out of a number of clauses linked together: *The burglar ran and I chased him because he stole my cake*. This sentence contains three clauses: 'The burglar ran', 'I chased him', 'he stole my cake'.

Clauses and phrases: the difference

Clauses include participants in an action denoted by a verb. Phrases, however, need not necessarily contain a verb. These phrases make little sense on their own: 'without a sound', 'very slowly indeed'. They work as part of a clause.

Simple, compound and complex sentences

The addition of clauses to single-clause sentences (simple sentences) can make multi-clause sentences (complex or compound sentences).

Simple sentences are made up of one clause, for example: *The dog barked*, *Sam was scared*.

Compound sentences are made up of clauses added to clauses. In compound sentences each of the clauses is of equal value; no clause is dependent on another. An example of a compound sentence is: *The dog barked and the parrot squawked*. Both these clauses are of equal importance: 'The dog barked', 'the parrot squawked'. Other compound sentences include, for example: *I like coffee and I like chocolate*, *I like coffee, but I don't like tea*.

Complex sentences are made up of a main clause with a subordinate clause or clauses. Subordinate clauses make sense in relation to the main clause. They say something about it and are dependent upon it, such as in the sentences: *The dog barked because he saw a burglar*; *Sam was scared so he phoned the police*.

In both these cases the subordinate clause ('he saw a burglar', 'he phoned the police') is elaborating on the main clause. They explain why the dog barked or why Sam was scared and, in doing so, are subordinate to those actions. The reader needs to see the main clauses to fully appreciate what the subordinate ones are stating.

Subject and object

The **subject** of a sentence or clause is the agent that performs the action denoted by the verb – ***Shaun** threw the ball*. The **object** is the agent to which the verb is done – 'ball'. It could be said that the subject does the verb to the object (a simplification but a useful one). The simplest type of sentence is known as the SVO (subject–verb–object) sentence (or clause), as in *You lost your way*, *I found the book* and *Lewis met Chloe*.

The active voice and the passive voice

These contrast two ways of saying the same thing:

Active voice	Passive voice
I found the book. Megan met Ben. The cow jumped over the moon.	The book was found by me. Ben was met by Megan. The moon was jumped over by the cow.

The two types of clause put the same subject matter in a different voice. Passive clauses are made up of a subject and verb followed by an agent.

The book	was found by	me.
subject	verb	agent
Ben	was met by	Megan.
subject	verb	agent

Sentences can be written in the active or the passive voice. A sentence can be changed from the active to the passive voice by:

- moving the subject to the end of the clause
- moving the object to the start of the clause
- changing the verb or verb phrase by placing a form of the verb 'be' before it (as in 'was found')
- changing the verb or verb phrase by placing 'by' after it.

In passive clauses the agent can be deleted, either because it does not need mentioning or because a positive choice is made to omit it. Texts on science may leave out the agent, with sentences such as *The water is added to the salt and stirred.*

4. Punctuation

Punctuation provides marks within sentences that guide the reader. Speech doesn't need punctuation (and would sound bizarre if it included noises for full stops and so on). In speech, much is communicated by pausing, changing tone and so on. In writing, the marks within and around a sentence provide indications of when to pause, when something is being quoted and so on.

Punctuation	Uses	Examples
A	**Capital letter** 1. Starts a sentence. 2. Indicates proper nouns. 3. Emphasises certain words.	1. All I want is cake. 2. You can call me Al. 3. I want it TOMORROW!
.	**Full stop** Ends sentences that are not questions or exclamations.	This is a sentence.
?	**Question mark** Ends a sentence that is a question.	Is this a question?
!	**Exclamation mark** Ends a sentence that is an exclamation.	Don't do that!
" " ' '	**Inverted commas (or quotation/ speech marks)** Encloses direct speech. Can be double or single.	"Help me," the man yelled. 'Help me,' the man yelled.
,	**Comma** 1. Places a pause between clauses within a sentence. 2. Separates items in a list. 3. Separates adjectives in a series. 4. Completely encloses clauses inserted in a sentence. 5. Marks speech from words denoting who said them.	1. We were late, although it didn't matter. 2. You will need eggs, butter and flour. 3. I wore a long, green, frilly skirt. 4. We were, after we had rushed to get there, late for the film. 5. 'Thank you,' I said.
-	**Hyphen** Connects elements of certain words.	Re-read, south-west.
:	**Colon** 1. Introduces lists (including examples). 2. Introduces summaries. 3. Introduces (direct) quotations. 4. Introduces a second clause that expands or illustrates the meaning of the first.	1. To go skiing these are the main items you will need: a hat, goggles, gloves and sunscreen. 2. We have learned the following on the ski slope: do a snow plough to slow down. 3. My instructor always says: 'Bend those knees.' 4. The snow hardened: it turned into ice.

Punctuation	Uses	Examples
;	**Semicolon** 1. Separates two closely linked clauses, and shows there is a link between them. 2. Separates items in a complex list.	1. On Tuesday, the bus was late; the train was early. 2. You can go by aeroplane, train and taxi; Channel tunnel train, coach, then a short walk; or aeroplane and car.
'	**Apostrophe of possession** Denotes the ownership of one thing by another (see page 159).	This is Mona's scarf. These are the teachers' books.
'	**Apostrophe of contraction** Shows the omission of a letter(s) when two (or occasionally more) words are contracted.	Don't walk on the grass.
...	**Ellipsis** 1. Shows the omission of words. 2. Indicates a pause.	1. The teacher moaned, 'Look at this floor… a mess… this class…' 2. Lou said: 'I think I locked the door… no, hang on, did I?'
( )	**Brackets** Contains a parenthesis – a word or phrase added to a sentence to give a bit more information.	The cupboard (which had been in my family for years) was broken.
–	**Dash** 1. Indicates additional information, with more emphasis than a comma. 2. Indicates a pause, especially for effect at the end of a sentence. 3. Contains extra information (used instead of brackets).	1. She is a teacher – and a very good one too. 2. We all know what to expect – the worst. 3. You finished that job – and I don't know how – before the deadline.

Adding an apostrophe of possession

The addition of an apostrophe can create confusion. The main thing to look at is the noun – ask:

- Is it singular or plural?
- Does it end in an 's'?

If the noun is singular and doesn't end in 's', you add an apostrophe and an 's', for example: *Indra's house* *the firefighter's bravery*	**If the noun is singular and ends in 's'**, you add an apostrophe and an 's', for example: *the bus's wheels* *Thomas's pen*
If the noun is plural and doesn't end in 's', you add an apostrophe and an 's', for example: *the women's magazine* *the geese's flight*	**If the noun is plural and ends in 's'**, you add an apostrophe but don't add an 's', for example: *the boys' clothes* *the dancers' performance*